T0266541

Breaking Ground on Your Memoir

Breaking Ground on Your Memoir

········●·········

Craft, Inspiration, and Motivation for Memoir Writers

Linda Joy Myers, PhD, and Brooke Warner

Creators of WriteYourMemoirInSixMonths.com

SHE WRITES PRESS

Published 2015
Printed in the United States of America
Interior design by Tabitha Lahr

Print ISBN: 978-1-63152-085-3
Digital ISBN: 978-1-63152-011-2

For information, address:
She Writes Press
1563 Solano Ave #546
Berkeley, CA 94707

She Writes Press is a division of SparkPoint Studio, LLC.

Contents

Introduction

Memoir writers often ask us what they can do to get the attention of an agent or publisher, hoping that if they've written a great memoir, someone will pick them up, ideally after the first query! We know how passionate memoir writers are about sharing their stories with the world, but we also know how much effort and time and practice it takes for writers to get their memoirs to a place where they're ready to be shopped to agents or editors, or to be published—traditionally or otherwise.

A memoir offers testimony and legacy, and it also invites readers into a world that may either be familiar or wholly different from their own; but either way, it must provide a mirror in which readers see themselves. For a memoir to become beloved, it must reach the heart of others; it must make a difference.

In order to write a memoir that illuminates your life experience, you need to have a combination of art and craft. The
art of memoir draws upon your memory and imagination,
your understanding of the past and how your story fits with
what you know about life. The art involves tapping into your
creativity and self-expression. Most writers who feel called
to write don't have too difficult a time tapping into the art
of writing, though sometimes what pours out is satisfying
and sometimes not. Then there's craft, which involves bringing the skills of good writing to your story in order to make
your memoir more vital and alive. These are skills that writers
must acquire, and must learn to recognize in others' work.
And memoir, while it employs many of the same techniques
as fiction, has some unique elements, particularly in narration and reflection, that we hope you will learn to adapt and
implement in your memoir, if you haven't already.

In this book, we present from the ground up—from basic to advanced—the skills you need to draw upon to write a
powerful and moving story. The book is peppered with the
motivation we all need when we start to hear that niggling
voice of doubt that wonders: *Can I really do all of this?* Writing any long-form work requires passion, accountability, and
a stick-to-itiveness that at times can be a challenge, but there
are always solutions. And we know you can do it. We're here
to help you believe—and then know—that you can, too.

Over the years, we've read, edited, assessed, and even
judged contest entries for countless memoirs. We see how even

when a writer has an interesting story, it can be hard to fully immerse ourselves in the world being presented to us, generally because the writer has unintentionally omitted or overlooked certain critical elements of craft. Sometimes this stems from the writer's not understanding certain elements of craft, sometimes a writer just doesn't have the confidence to execute what they know they should, and sometimes it's a classic case of not knowing what they don't know. All successful memoir writers need to deepen their commitment to learning how to write scenes, how to choose the structure that best suits their book, and how to carry ideas and themes all the way through to a satisfying conclusion. There are multiple layers to writing a powerful story, and in this book we have included the tools to help you write a solid draft of your book, along with the elements you will need to revise and edit your work toward the end goal of having a publish-ready manuscript.

We have also included throughout this book many examples of writing from best-selling memoirists to showcase certain elements of craft and how to do it right. We encourage you to read and to take classes, and to remember that this journey you're on, though it might at times feel like more than you signed on for, will ultimately be one of the most rewarding of your life. Come along with us to break ground on your memoir and to gain and hone the skills necessary to tend to it, gently and intentionally, until it becomes the beautiful gift in the world you envisioned it would be when the seed of the idea first emerged. We invite you to learn and to be inspired, and where you feel like you already have a handle on something, then just celebrate! There is so much to know, and you get to pat yourself on the back for those things you already know you're doing well. And if everything feels new, then that's just fine, too. Wherever you are in your journey is where you are, and we are honored that you chose our book to be a support along the way. So let's begin!

CHAPTER 1

Getting Grounded

How do we begin this amazing journey we call memoir writing? Your life is complex; there are so many stories to tell, and it can be difficult to decide what to include and what to leave out. Because of this, it's easy for fledgling memoirists to leave their memoirs floating in the air, suspended from the earth, with nothing to anchor them. But everything you have experienced has taken place at a certain time and in a particular location, and it's crucial to ground your memoir in those moments—and in the message you want to share.

The difference between writing just for yourself and writing for an audience—which is what you're doing when you write a memoir—is the difference between writing in your journal and writing a book. There is absolutely real value in simply getting your writing out onto the page in any form, of course, but if you believe that there is a readership for your book, you will eventually need to sit down and sift through your story in an outwardly focused way. Ultimately, this process all comes down to figuring out your theme, message, and scope—and doing that starts with getting grounded.

To us, getting grounded means getting centered and getting connected with your story. Too many writers just jump in without thinking about what it is that they want to say or how they want to say it. In order to avoid falling into this trap and ending up spinning your wheels indefinitely, you need to figure out what focus your memoir will have.

FIGURING OUT YOUR CATEGORY

If you're writing memoir, your genre, of course, is memoir. There are subgenres of memoir, categories and types, and understanding which one(s) your memoir belongs to is vital.

Deciding which category best fits the theme of your memoir is a subjective choice, and you may find that your memoir belongs in a few different subcategories. But it's important that your memoir not try to broach all of the categories—that it not be a spiritual memoir that is also a humor memoir that is also a travel memoir that is also a coming-of-age memoir, for example. If you feel your memoir does span multiple categories in this way, there's probably too much going on in your story, and you need to find a sharper focus.

You may know exactly what you're doing—or trying to do—and if that's the case, good for you! But for many writers, this isn't the case. They're trying to get their book to be too many things—perhaps because they don't understand how valuable it is to pick a specific subgenre and stick to it, or perhaps because they find it difficult to make a decision about what kind of book they're writing. If this is you, know that figuring out your category will ground you in what it is that you are currently doing and what it is that you actually *want* to do.

So let's touch upon what some of these categories are, starting with coming-of-age memoir. This is very straightforward; usually these kinds of memoirs start when someone is around four or five years old and end in the teenage years. A classic example would be Augusten Burroughs's *Running with Scissors*. Some people might say that Jeannette Walls's *The Glass Castle* is also a coming-of-age memoir, but we place memoirs like these—stories that deal with difficult childhoods and/or abusive situations—in the transformation/survivor memoir category. This is where some subjectivity is going to play a role.

Another big category is life-experience memoirs. These are memoirs about motherhood, career, inspiring tales, extraordinary stories—for example, *Between a Rock and a Hard Place*, by Aron Ralston, who had to cut off his own arm to escape a life-or-death situation. Obviously that's a very extraordinary story, but life-experience memoirs don't have to be about something so extreme; they can be ordinary-life-event stories, too.

Then there are relationship memoirs—stories that deal

with love, dating, divorce, friendship. These are very popular kinds of memoirs. A great example of a story that fits here is *Truth and Beauty*, Ann Patchett's memoir about her friendship with Lucy Grealy, which was a best seller.

There are other categories as well (see the sidebar at the end of this chapter), but the point is, your readers need to be able to wrap their minds around what your story is. The minute you start saying that your story is about ten different things, it quickly becomes something that is just too much for your readers to process. So if you have more than six or seven subgenres that you can fit your book into, you want to begin to reconceptualize what it is that you're writing and start to narrow your focus. Take note that memoir, by definition, presents a slice of life. It is different from autobiography in this way. A fellow memoir teacher once described it this way to us: *Autobiography is the story of a life; memoir is a story from a life*. It's an important distinction.

A lot of writers go too big or take on too much in a single memoir because they think, *Well, the more outrageous my story is, the better*—and to some extent this is true, in the sense that a lot of memoirs that are either extraordinary or dysfunctional or wild in some way get a lot of attention. Many readers want to be transported; they want to experience something that is different from their lives. You need to be able to walk a fine line of recognizing where and how to rein in your own story. That starts with figuring out your category—and then figuring out your turning points.

TURNING POINTS

All of us have lived many moments, but not all of those moments are especially significant—and not all of them belong in our stories. Finding our turning points in life, moments of change, is how we grab hold of the important moments that belong in our memoir. They're like little hooks, and they're the foundation of any memoir. Turning points turn into scenes; scenes turn into a collection of scenes; and those collections of scenes, woven together with narration, turn into chapters. Simply put, this is how you build a memoir: by stringing together a series of turning points.

Writing a memoir, then, begins with figuring out what turning points you will include in your story. You can begin by brainstorming freely—by writing down as many turning points as you can come up with that you think might be relevant to your story. Some will be hugely significant; others will be less so, but they may be important to include, whether for context or for narrative continuity. Don't worry too much about that initially. The big thing here is to get them down where you can look at them and sort through them.

Once you have a list of your turning points in front of you, you may start to feel overwhelmed by how much is there. What we recommend is that you try to cut your list down to around ten to fifteen turning points. *Ten to fifteen points?* you're thinking. *I can't do that!* We know it sounds difficult, but you absolutely can—and you need to. You'll never get past that sense of being overwhelmed if you have fifty or one hundred items on your list. So think about your theme; think about what you really want to get across in your story. Then ask yourself, *Of all the turning points I wrote down, which ones are the most relevant to my theme?* Keep the most important ones, and discard the rest. (For now, anyway. It's okay if you want to add some of them back in further down the line, but you want to start with only the essentials.)

This exercise is valuable for all memoirists, but especially for those who aren't really clear about where they should start their story. That's an important thing to think about before you start writing: where your story starts and where it ends. More often than not, we find that most people's scope is too big. We frequently see people start at some point—age five, age seven, age ten—and go all the way to later in life. Some people can keep the focus needed for a memoir, but most will veer into autobiography territory. You may find when you're looking at the turning points you've come up with that they are actually mapping out your autobiography, not your memoir. So it's your job to choose which ones belong not in the story of your whole life, but in the story you're trying to tell right now (and remember, many of you may have more than one memoir in you; maybe you can save some of these turning points for use in your next book!).

What you'll find when you start to think about your turning points, noting which ones to include in your memoir, is that there's a wealth of information in your life to choose from. You can approach your story from a particular place, such as themes that had a pattern like abuse or love relationships—or you can turn the angle ever so slightly and enter from a completely different place, perhaps themes that occur over decades. So there's a bit of an experience of expansion and contraction here. We think it's valuable to understand this, because people can easily become limited and small in their thinking, and what your turning points do is open up vast possibilities—and then you can go small again as you develop your focus and theme. The turning points help you to get a broader perspective on your overall story, but because they are specific moments, they also help you focus when you start to think about writing your scenes and turning them into chapters.

SCENES:
The Building Blocks of Memoir

If you want to write memoir, it's critical that you understand how to write a scene. A scene draws upon your turning points, and it is up to you to decide which moments are important enough to "show" in a scene." At the beginning of your book, you'll be introducing people, including yourself, as characters. There's movement and action in a scene, and sensual details, such as smells, sounds, and visual imagery. You'll use description to paint a picture of where you were when things happened, and to place the reader there as well. You'll include a kinesthetic sense of feeling and texture in your scenes, like the difference between the way snow feels under your boots and how a hot, humid day feels when you're down to shorts and a sleeveless top. The end of a scene will often include a narrative passage that relates to what happened in the scene, a reflection that prompts the reader to consider the larger ramifications of your internal experience. This is the essence of takeaway, which is the result of good scene writing.

Consider the following points when you write your scenes:

- **Place and setting**—landscape, time of year, weather, towns vs. cities, etc.
- **Characters**—characters in action and dialogue
- **Situation**—what is the situation or problem?
- **Action**—how do different people in your scene react, move, respond?
- **Dialogue**—how do people talk (including body language)?
- **Conflict**—how do people express their differences?
- **Context; time in history**—when does the story occur in time?
- **Sensual details**—how does the world feel, smell, taste, sound?

Scenes are like the beads on a necklace of your larger narration. Think of a scene as a single moment in time that anchors your reader to a place that's full of sensory details, like a cold winter morning in New England, sitting on the bleachers at your high school football stadium, smoking a cigarette. This is the anchor, and from that point you can move forward in a linear way, or you can flash back, departing from the "current" timeline to create more depth of understanding. Don't forget to conclude your scenes. If you depart from your scene with reflection, come back! Make sure if you move forward in time that you show it, so that we don't end up stuck with you out on those high school bleachers while you've moved along to college. As a rule of thumb, each scene builds connection, understanding, and a felt sense of the moment in your memoir. Scenes build chapters, and chapters build your book.

TIMELINE

Once you have your list of turning points compiled, you want to create a timeline. You can have a sense of humor and make it go all the way from zero to one hundred, or you can make it shorter—but keep in mind that your memoir is most likely going to be focused within a certain time frame in your theme, and you're going to want to stay within that time frame. So if you do a timeline for your whole life, you'll need to do a second one that focuses down on a smaller time period as you begin to get clear on your theme and messages.

Draw out your timeline on a large piece of paper or a poster board—something big enough to fit the time period you're covering in one, continuous line. Use a pencil so you can make changes. Draw a horizontal line to represent the passage of time in your life, putting your starting date at the left side of the chart and your ending date on the right side. Divide the line in between into decades (or months, if you're covering only a year or two), then map out your turning points by drawing vertical lines out from the appropriate places in the timeline, drawing a bubble at the end of each one and writing your turning points in those bubbles.

Get creative with this thing. Use colored pencils. Take your time charting your turning points. As you do, you'll find that certain memories will spur other memories. Not only will you start thinking about what happened in the moments you're mapping out, but you'll notice the insights you gained during those moments, the meaning they have for you now. The more fun you can make this exercise—using different colors and images, even listening to music that inspires you or brings you back to the time that you want to write about—the better.

This exercise isn't always fun, of course: if you're writing about really hard topics, it can be difficult to travel back to some of these spaces, but it's important to do so. Once you get into this creative mapping, it can be very engaging and sometimes even exciting. Because it's a visual representation of what your story is—where you were, where you are now— and of what your message is, it can also give you a lot more insight into what you want to say.

Sometimes people have a clear sense of where their story begins but no sense of where it ends. If this is your situation, whether you're writing something that spans thirty years or one year, creating a timeline is great because it can often help you see how much rearranging of things you need to do and what needs to be sacrificed. Starting by "backing into" your memoir—establishing where it ends before you even figure out where it begins—can be game-changing.

SCOPE & THEME

So you've thought about what category your memoir belongs in; you've figured out your turning points; you've made your timeline. Now that these elements that ground you in your story are in place, do you have a better handle on what you want to write about? Do you understand what it is you're taking on?

Let's say you've mapped out your memoir. You know where it starts and where it ends. You've narrowed it down to a particular slice of your life, or you've homed in on your theme. The next thing to consider is how to hold all that happened during this period within a container of sorts. It's not enough to write the details of what happened to you. If your story is simply a statement of facts and plot points—*this happened, this happened, and then this happened in my life*—it doesn't matter how fascinating a life you might have lived. It's still got to be contained by your themes. Your theme (or themes, in some cases) is the lens through which you are telling your story, and that lens has to be apparent to the reader.

Take addiction memoirs, which are an easy type of memoir to wrap your mind around because they typically start by showcasing the addiction and how it impacts the author's life. Then the narrator moves through the addiction to the other side of addiction, and ends with transformation and healing. That creates an obvious arc. What you'll notice in memoirs like these is that they never lose sight of the *what*—which, in this case, is addiction (how addiction impacts the narrator's life, and how they're overcoming it).

If you look at any thematic memoir, the *what* is always that concise. Your *what* really shouldn't be, "Oh, well, I grew up in Kansas and then I moved to California because I wanted to pursue acting, but that didn't work out, and so then I moved to Washington and had kids and then my kids got married." That's not a memoir; that is an autobiography, and if you try to pitch a work like this as a memoir to an agent or an editor, they are almost definitely not going to bite—not unless you are very, very famous.

Keep in mind that when we talk about scope, we're talking about entry points—where the reader enters your story and where they leave it. Let's go back to the memoir that starts with you as a young child and ends with you at sixty, and say you choose to go from age twenty-five to age fifty instead. That choice doesn't mean you can't talk about your childhood; you can absolutely flash back to various scenes from your youth and show how those experiences have affected you. There is freedom of movement in these shorter time frames. What we're saying is that the more you can confine that linear story of point A to point B, and then use techniques like flashbacks or add certain important memories to give some of the background where it makes sense to do so, the better.

There are, of course, some exceptions to the rule. For example, Linda Joy's memoir, *Don't Call Me Mother,* covers a lot of time, but it works because it's thematically very tight—it's about three generations of mothers who abandoned their daughters, and how Linda Joy broke that chain of abandonment. But in order to get it to where it is now, she had to cut out 55,000 words—almost the length of a book—from the original manuscript. She hadn't taken a memoir-writing class before she started writing it; she had begun, as so many authors do, without knowing what she was doing. So it was only after she had written this long, meandering manuscript that she became clear on the arc and theme and then had to go back and take out everything that didn't relate to it. In other words, she had to do things the hard way.

As you conceptualize the structure of your memoir, you're going to do yourself a favor if you keep your scope to a manageable length. When it comes to writing memoir, the old truism "less is more" really does apply.

. . . .

Playing with Time

There are lots of different ways to handle time in your memoir. We won't say that one way is right and one way is wrong, because there are various choices you can make. What we will say, however, is that you must keep the reader alongside you the whole way through—wherever you go, you have to leave enough markers along the way so they don't get lost between jumps.

Jeannette Walls covers a lot of ground in *The Glass Castle.* She starts as an adult, then goes back to when she was three, and then, after proceeding through her childhood bit by bit, she makes another big jump forward again. Her structure is a bit complicated, but she pulls it off because she adheres to her themes the whole way through, and she always makes it clear what's happening and when it happened—she makes it easy for the reader to follow along.

Another way to collapse or move quickly through time is to use part breaks. There are memoirs, for instance, where Part One deals with getting married and having a first child, and then Part Two opens ten years later: the oldest kid is ten, and there are a bunch of younger siblings as well now, the parents are not doing well, things are falling apart, etc. You can do that—you can skip huge chunks of time, even decades. But when you do, you need to make sure you do an effective job of painting a picture of what life is like—then and now—and getting the reader up to speed. Ultimately, it's all about keeping your audience engaged, and that requires keeping them grounded.

. . . .

THE WHEN & THE WHY

We're talking a lot about managing time on a broader scale; now let's zoom in on how to approach time in specific scenes. We find that many authors we work with frequently make the mistake of forgetting to ground the reader (and maybe even themselves) in the *when* of a scene.

In the fuzziness of our memories, it's easy to say, "Well, I have this memory and it's kind of floating in my mind, so I'll just write it down that way." But when you're translating turning points into scenes, each of those scenes happened in a certain place at a certain time, and it's important to be specific about them. If you don't know exactly where or when, it's okay to guess. If you can't remember whether something happened in 1985 or 1986, for example—it probably doesn't matter that much. You can just pick one. But 1985 is a different era and stage of development than 1995—and that difference matters. In 1995 you were ten years older—you were thinking different things and having different experiences than you would have had in 1985, and it's important that you give time markers to the reader so that they're not guessing or lost.

In order to drill down to the *when* of your memoir, you may need to do some research about the time period you're writing about, or dig through old photos or journals, something to jog your memory. Sometimes you'll simply be able to make some educated guesses. Perhaps your timeline will help you sort out some of the details. Choose whatever will help you to pin down specific moments in time.

Once you've figured out your *when*, the second thing you should asking yourself is *why*. Why were you there? Why is it important? You'll want to do this with every scene. As we've said, some turning points will be hugely significant—big moments where something transitional or transformational happens in your life. Other scenes will be less important, less crucial to your growth throughout the book, but you still need to ask yourself these same questions. If you can't come up with a satisfactory answer for why you're including a scene and why it's important to your memoir as a whole, then it probably shouldn't be in your book.

THE WHO & THE WHAT

The *who* and the *what* come right on the heels of the *when* and the *why*. To some extent, the *who* is more obvious: it's about making sure that you're clear on who your characters are and what their purpose is. Pretty straightforward. The *what*, though, is much bigger, and it operates on different levels. There's the *what* of the characters (What are they doing? What do they want?), but there's also the *what* of the chapter (What is the point of your scene? What is the point of your chapter?).

Before you start writing your memoir, you need to have a conversation with yourself about the *what* of your book. What is it about? What are you trying to say? You want your answers to these questions to be clear and concise. There should be a clear takeaway for the reader, and you should be able to communicate what that takeaway is. (We have a whole section about takeaway later in the book; it's another critically important element of memoir writing.) For now, if you can explain what your memoir is about in three sentences, you're in good shape. Eventually, though, you'll want to hone it down to a single sentence (your hook)—and the sooner you can start to articulate that, the better.

INTENTION:
The Character vs. The Narrator

Memoir is unique in regards to other types of nonfiction because you present your story from two different perspectives. In your memoir, you are both the narrator telling the story— the voice guiding the reader through scenes, reflections, and takeaways—and a character in the story, the protagonist. And this means you are writing from two different perspectives with at least two intentions.

As you write your memoir, you have to think about yourself as you would any other character in a story. In fiction-writing classes—memoir borrows from the tools of fiction to create a good story—the question that's asked is always "What do the characters want, and how is their desire being thwarted?" This is a question of intention.

As you think about intention, try not to write only from your head—dig deeper. We are embodied creatures; we experience life through our physical bodies. It's important to understand the ways in which you bring yourself to the page as the character, you in the scene, the embodied you who lived at that time. Think about what it was like to be in your body in the scenes you write. For example, your house may have felt enormous to you as a young child, but then later you went back to visit that house and noticed it was actually quite small. Those are two different aspects of you: child you and adult you. How do you write about them from different perspectives? How do you show up, authentically, as both?

There are a few memoirs that embody only the child narrator. When you do this, you are adopting what Sue William Silverman, author of *Fearless Confessions*, calls the "voice of innocence," where you're wholly and completely that child or fifteen-year-old or twenty-five-year-old and you never become the "now" narrator. But most memoirs use both the narrator voice (the "voice of experience") and the character voice (the "voice of innocence"), which requires being able to fluctuate between the intention of the narrator and the intention of the character.

Oftentimes the voice of experience is done in reflection (e.g., "I couldn't have understood this at the time, but . . ."). This allows you to look back at the person you were at that time and make some sense of the decisions you made or the experience you were going through. This intention, coming in as the narrative voice, gives you the opportunity to offer up wisdom that wasn't available to you at the time you're writing about.

As the narrator, then, you are responsible for reflecting, guiding, and showing emotional responses. It's almost like "you the character" is the body, and "you the narrator" is the mind. Framing it this way makes it easier to understand that when it comes to "you the character," the important thing to remember is the physicality of the character and what they're experiencing, whereas when it comes to "you the narrator," it's all about reflection and takeaway (which refers to what your reader is getting from reading your book, or what message you're imparting).

It may feel difficult to write with the voice of experience if the events you're relating didn't happen very long ago—for example, you may be writing right up into the present moment, or up until just a few years ago. Regardless of how much actual time has passed since the events you're relating occurred, you need to look for opportunities to show the reader something that the "you" of those moments would not have had the objectivity to express. You're in the emotions of that moment as the character, but as the narrator you have to be the one who is pulling the reader through those scenes in a way that provides some perspective.

We're not saying this is easy; it isn't. It's a difficult thing to master. It's sort of like singing and dancing and eating a hot dog at the same time: you're doing many things at once, and you have to work to find a balance. The more you can harness the power of entering your story as both the narrator and the character, the more in control of the choices you're making you'll feel. These are your tools, and you get to decide which ones to use at any given moment. Think of it as a home improvement project: you would much rather have a hammer *and* a screwdriver than just a hammer if you're trying to put something together, right? Well, the same goes for writing a book. The more tools you have at your disposal, the better and freer you'll feel.

. . . .

How do you deal with writing about memories of trauma that you repressed as a child but remembered as an adult?

By "deal with," we mean how do you write these difficult memories? You begin by deciding what point of view you're going to use. Are you going to write these memories mostly through the narrator's window, which means looking back at it in small chunks, or are you going to write from the point of view of the child, perhaps chronologically, all the way through? If there's a lot of trauma in your story, it can feel daunting to stay in those traumatic memories for very long, particularly if you're still triggered by what you experienced. To distance yourself from the intensity, you can have the narrator looking back, and go back and forth in time. This offers you the opportunity to weave in and out of the traumatic experience. Not everyone does this, however; in her book *Blackbird,* Jennifer Lauck writes about being a desperately lost child who's suffering all the way through the book in one form or another. She stays in that child's point of view and embodies that child all the way. When we read it, we are inside that child's body and experiencing everything from her point of view.

We recommend reading other memoirists who have done what you're trying to do. *When the Piano Stops,* by Catherine McCall, is an abuse memoir and very powerful, but a lot of the memories she writes about in her book were repressed until she was an adult. If this is an experience you've had, you might have some fear about sharing those memories because they seem dangerous or painful to think about. Many people have grown up being taught not to talk about what happened in the family and to keep personal matters private. Some families make it clear that if you speak about anything shameful, you will be punished. It's important to remember that the memories you have belong to you. You get to write about them, but it might take a little while to get to the point where you feel you have given yourself complete permission to write your story. Getting to a place of permission might involve support from others, which is why we believe in the power of finding a sacred space that's safe for you, either with a teacher or coach or in a writing partnership or group. It's important that you feel comfortable sharing your personal story with an intimate, protected audience before you go out and publish your book for the world to see.

What matters most is your experience and your interpretation of that experience. It can be challenging to write about traumatic memories if there are still family members in your life who might dispute your story, but stay with it. Stand strong. What really matters in memoir is your interpretation of events. You can speculate on what your mother's interpretation might have been, or your uncle's, but all that matters in your story is that you are discovering and presenting your own truth. Families always have different versions of the same story. Part of writing trauma can be claiming or reclaiming what happened to you and bringing it out of hiding. The more you can do this with an eye toward helping the reader to understand your lived experience, the better. We recommend writing traumatic memories in small doses, for only fifteen or twenty minutes, then stopping, to limit how much of the dark story you have to face at once. If you feel yourself dissociating or feeling scared, back off, take a break, and come back later. You might try writing a happier story then for balance.

. . . .

GET OUT THE MAP

Hurling yourself into your story can be good; you can absolutely get a lot done that way, and freewriting is important (we'll talk more about this in Chapter 2). But if your story starts to feel too big—if you wander too far or too long—it's easy to get stuck or thrown completely off course. We have worked with countless memoirists who have spent months, or even years, working on their books endlessly, without any real sense of what they're doing. They're just kind of swimming in it. After a while, that becomes exhausting and frustrating and completely defeating. But if you take that passion that you started out with and apply it toward taking the proper steps to prepare yourself—if you train yourself, just as you would train for a marathon or a new job or any other important endeavor—your whole experience of writing your memoir is going to be a lot better and a whole lot more fulfilling.

Your memoir is a living, breathing thing; it wants to be written, and it already knows what it wants to be. You're the person who gets to guide it there—to mold it and shape it into what it needs to become. Spending some time mapping and conceptualizing and really homing in on what your story is will save you a lot of pain in the long run. Lay down the proper groundwork, and everything else will fall into place.

MEMOIR CATEGORIES

Childhood, Adolescent, and Coming-of-Age Memoirs

- Family dynamics, dysfunction, drama
- Unique childhood experiences/growing-up stories
- School days

Examples of this type of memoir include: *Running with Scissors*, by Augusten Burroughs; *Jesus Land*, by Julia Scheeres; *I'm Down*, by Mishna Wolff; *Funny in Farsi*, by Firoozeh Dumas.

Life-Experience Memoirs

- Motherhood
- Career
- Incarceration
- Extraordinary stories
- Inspiring tales
- Disease: living with, witnessing, surviving
- Death: witnessing, questioning, living in the aftermath

Examples of this type of memoir include: *It Sucked and Then I Cried*, by Heather Armstrong; *Battle Hymn of the Tiger Mother*, by Amy Chua; *My Life Deleted*, by Scott Bolzan; *Between a Rock and a Hard Place*, by Aron Ralston; *Reading Lolita in Tehran*, by Azar Nafisi; *The Year of Magical Thinking*, by Joan Didion.

Relationships

- Love
- Dating
- Divorce
- Friendship
- Animal stories

Examples of this type of memoir include: *Truth and Beauty*, by Ann Patchett; *The Girl's Guide to Homelessness*, by Brianna Karp; *Happens Every Day*, by Isabel Gillies; *31 Dates in 31 Days*, by Tamara Duricka Johnson; *Marley & Me*, by John Grogan.

Cultural/Ethnic/Sexuality Memoirs

- Coming-out stories
- Stories of growing up within a particular culture
- African American, Asian American, Southeast Asian–specific stories, where race and ethnicity play a primary role in the story

Examples of this type of memoir include: *Black, White, & Jewish*, by Rebecca Walker; *Bitch Is the New Black*, by Helena Andrews; *YELL-Oh! Girls!*, edited by Vickie Nam.

Food Memoirs

- Cooking
- Eating
- Inspired by food
- Gardening
- Food-movement stories

Examples of this type of memoir include: *Julie and Julia*, by Julie Powell; *Tender at the Bone*, by Ruth Reichl; *The Fortune Cookie Chronicles*, by Jennifer 8. Lee; *Farm City*, by Novella Carpenter; *Licking the Spoon*, by Candace Walsh.

Travel Memoirs

- Single destination
- Multiple destinations
- Theme-based travel
- Soul-searching travel

Examples of this type of memoir include: *Eat, Pray, Love*, by Elizabeth Gilbert; *The Road to Somewhere*, by James A. Reeves; *The Adventures of Bindi Girl*, by Erin Reese; *Es Cuba*, by Lea Aschkenas.

Survivor Memoirs

- Harrowing childhood stories
- War stories
- Abuse (sexual, physical, or emotional)
- Trafficking
- Prostitution

Examples of this type of memoir include: *The Glass Castle*, by Jeannette Walls; *The Tender Bar*, by J. R. Moehringer; *A Child Called "It,"* by Dave J. Pelzer; *A Piece of Cake*, by Cupcake Brown.

Addiction and Compulsion Memoirs

- Drug or alcohol abuse
- Smoking
- Parents of child with drug or alcohol problem
- Eating disorders
- Body dysmorphia

Examples of this type of memoir include: *Beautiful Boy*, by David Sheff; *Tweak*, by Nic Sheff; *Lit*, by Mary Karr; *A Life in Smoke*, by Julia Hansen; *Drinking, A Love Story*, by Caroline Knapp; *Purge*, by Nicole Johns; *Fat Girl*, by Judith Moore.

Emotion Memoirs
- Stories of a single emotion
- Personal interactions with things like time, money, etc.

Examples of this type of memoir include: *Monkey Mind*, by Daniel Smith; *Money, A Memoir*, by Liz Perle; *Dancing at the Shame Prom*, edited by Amy Ferris and Hollye Dexter.

Spirituality Memoirs
- Spiritual development
- Your experiences with religion
- Finding or losing religion

Examples of this type of memoir include: *Traveling Mercies*, by Anne Lamott; *The Spiral Staircase*, by Karen Armstrong; *Unorthodox*, by Deborah Feldman; *90 Minutes in Heaven*, by Don Piper.

Other Memoirs
- Humor (*Me Talk Pretty One Day*, by David Sedaris)
- Hybrids (*The Pain Chronicles*, by Melanie Thernstrom)
- Graphic memoirs (*Are You My Mother?*, by Alison Bechdel)
- Anything extraordinarily unique that doesn't fit into the above-mentioned categories
- Personal-essay anthologies that do not fit into the above-mentioned categories

CHAPTER 2

Building Your Framework

Many memoirists don't have a process or a plan. They simply start writing—and keep writing, and keep writing. This kind of freewriting can certainly open up a lot of possibilities for you, and it can be a *part* of your process (we'll get to that later in this chapter, in fact), but it can't be your whole process. Freewriting is a great way to start something, but it's not a viable way to finish anything. In order to complete your memoir and end up with something polished and cohesive, you're going to need more: you're going to need framing and structure.

You may be very early in the memoir-writing process, and if that's the case, it may not be the right time for you to start getting into the nitty-gritty of outlining yet. You might need to spend more time on the timeline exercise we discussed in Chapter 1 and process what happened and how you feel about it before moving forward. But if you've been processing and freewriting for more than five or six months, and you know you want to write a memoir, it's time to dive in and start making some real decisions about where to go next.

WHY YOU NEED FRAMING & STRUCTURE

Framing and structure are solid and concrete ways to help you compartmentalize your story. Together, they help you to create a container for everything you're writing—though within that container there are endless variations and opportunities for you to be creative and to have fun with the process. Some writers fear that if their story is too structured or if they're following an outline, they won't be allowed to go down the rabbit hole of their creative process. They get hooked into this idea that they're not going to be able to write their vision of the story, and think that adhering to a frame will rob them of flexibility with their voice. We're here to say that this is not the case. We would argue, in fact, that you actually have *more* freedom when you create a frame and structure for yourself, because it allows you to be less linear while keeping your end goal in sight. You can still go down the rabbit hole and be as creative as you like. The real difference is that you'll end up with a whole lot more usable material.

Linda Joy coined the term "the muddy middle"—where you get into the middle of your story and you're looking forward and you're looking back and you're thinking, *Oh, jeez, where have I been and where am I going?* The muddy middle is a place where many memoirists hang out for a very long time (sometimes it starts as early as Chapter 2 and follows you to the last couple of chapters), and it is not a particularly fun place to be. But framing and structure are your ticket out of the muddy middle. When you have a sense of what the parameters of your memoir are from the beginning, you understand your direction—which means you're less likely to hit that wall of not knowing what's supposed to happen next.

MEMOIR STRUCTURE OPTIONS

The linear memoir is probably the most popular type of memoir written today. It's the most straightforward, and the structure we most commonly recommend for first-time authors, but there are a handful of other possibilities to consider as well. Here are some of the structures we've seen in memoir. Your job is to figure out what resonates most with you and then read other authors who've executed what you're hoping to accomplish.

Linear

As we said, this is the most common kind of structure you'll see. A linear narrative goes from Point A to Point B along the continuum of your life over a certain period of time. When you write a linear memoir, you want to know where you're starting and where you're ending. Frank McCourt's *Angela's Ashes* is a beautifully executed linear memoir. It starts even before he's born, with the story of his parents having met, destined for ruin, and ends when he's nineteen years old, returning from Ireland, where he grew up, to America, where he was born. This is a classic coming-of-age journey, though it might start a big younger (prebirth) than most. Note that you want to figure out a good time frame for your work that doesn't span your entire life. Remember, memoir is not autobiography, and it should span anywhere from one year to twenty years, though there are of course exceptions to this general rule.

What's important here is that you have a solid handle on what time period you're covering. Even if the time period is on the longer side, you need to remember one thing: it's not going to be your entire life. Remember, as we said in Chapter 1, memoir is a story *from* a life, not the story *of* a life. You don't want to inadvertently turn your memoir into an autobiography. Many writers get anxious about what they perceive to be the limitations of a certain time frame, like the notion that twenty years should be a maximum number of years to cover in your memoir. But consider this: If you're writing a memoir that spans ages forty to fifty, you are not barred from writing about your childhood. You just need to consider a different structure, which is the "framed memoir" we're going to explain next.

Framed

The framed memoir has become an increasingly popular form of memoir for its flexibility and because it allows to you write along a linear continuum, from point A to point B, yet offers an opportunity to jump back and forward in your life through the use of flashback and memory, and future and conditional tenses. Those two points—the beginning and the end—encompass a segment of time that can be as short as a few months and as long as a decade or two. Deciding what your memoir frame will be, then, requires that you answer one question: *Where does my story start, and where does it end?*

An excellent example of this type of memoir is Cheryl Strayed's *Wild*, which takes place over the course of a three-month journey on the Pacific Crest Trail, but also shows scenes from her past in flashback. As we've noted, your frame can be much longer than a few months—it can be several years. It's up to you to decide what part of your story you want to cover.

Beyond the necessity of a bookended time frame, the idea of a framed memoir is that you are taking the reader through an important or transitional time in your life. From Point A to Point B, you want to show personal transformation of some sort; the protagonist—you—needs to change and grow and learn, and in essence by the end of your story be a different version of who you were at the beginning. Showing transformation, and the threads of your life that are part of this kind of change, generally requires offering up backstory. The backstory happens within the frame—Point A to Point B—through the use of flashback and memory. Your challenge is to look for entry points along the linear timeline of Point A to Point B that allow you to jump around in time and shed some light on those past events that have been significant to your life. It's a bit like traveling down a staircase into your past, then popping back up into the "current" timeline when you're finished reexperiencing that memory. Flashbacks bring new knowledge to illuminate the present story line.

Some writers actually include so much memory and flashback that their memoirs are mostly about the past, even though their frame covers a more recent timeline. You can do this by including full flashback chapters, or by including flashback scenes within a current chapter, which work wonderfully when handled properly. You can even flash forward if you want to—using the conditional voice to foreshadow for the reader what's to come (e.g., "I couldn't have known it then, but later I would discover that . . ."). In essence, the frame setup gives you a starting point and an ending point, but within that frame you are looking for opportunities to tell your backstory. *Wild* is one of the best examples we know of a memoir that skillfully weaves back and forth in time. There are many ways to move through time within the frame you choose; you just have to make sure always to find your way back to your linear timeline at some point, to pick back up where you left off. This approach is great for many writers because it gives you permission to go back in time as much as you want without being too messy about it.

Circular

Framed memoirs are not the only type of memoir you can write, of course. The circular story is another structure some writers use, and it's one with fewer concrete rules about the end and the beginning: it goes back and forth through time constantly and may even be told in voices other than your own. A famous example is Maxine Hong Kingston's *Woman Warrior*—a beautiful book. Of course, there are many who argue that *Woman Warrior*, because of its circular and experimental nature, is not memoir at all. Kingston moves around in time and mythology and voice throughout the book, and though by the end you do have a story, it's not a linear one. But Kingston refers to it as a memoir, and she's certainly not the only person to have written creative nonfiction in this circular style.

Braided

Braided memoirs give writers an opportunity to create two parallel timelines—a past and a present. There are many ways to braid. You can braid every other chapter—past, present, past, present—or you can braid within chapters, being conscientious of your scenes and having some in the past and some in the present. Switching back and forth every other chapter is a more controlled experience and can be a better choice for a first-time author. An example of a braided memoir is Michael Datcher's *Raising Fences: A Black Man's Love Story*, in which the author alternates between the "then" and the "now" narrator throughout the book. The braided memoir is a good solution for those authors who feel that they are writing about adult life but want childhood experiences to play a central role in their narrative.

Association

Association is a style of memoir writing where, rather than using a linear timeline or even a frame, you simply use association to move through your book. Sometimes there might be a loose timeline you're following, but instead of thinking so much about time to propel you forward, you might instead be relying upon turning points and other events to bounce around thematically.

In her book *Devotion*, Dani Shapiro uses this kind of style to create a mosaic of her experience of faith. The book is a spiritual journey of sorts, though it's really just about her life and the choices she made along the way. It's a soft, subtle, and beautifully executed memoir that feels like an exploration. Rather than following a particularly structured trajectory, Shapiro seems to dance with what comes up, as if she were following her intuition and associations along the way. This is why we call this style association, because you're allowing the windows of your experience to choose where you take your reader next. You need to be a skilled writer in order to accomplish this structure, as it's the least structured way of writing a memoir and it's easy to get lost and messy when you write this way. For people who are not fans of structure and who are writing a very thematic book (like *Devotion*, or Caroline Knapp's *Drinking, A Love Story*), this can be a satisfying (though challenging) endeavor.

Experimental

Experimental memoirs are those that don't follow the rules of convention. Just because these structures exist doesn't mean that you have to have a certain kind of structure for your memoir. We recommend finding a clear structure only because we've seen too many memoirists get to Chapter 3 or 4 of their book and feel like they are stuck and don't know how to move forward in the story. This generally happens because they don't know where they're going, and it's the point where many aspiring memoirists realize they need a structure if they're ever going to complete their book.

Brooke has worked with a handful of experimental memoirs over the years, and they certainly can and do work. One example is *Purge: Rehab Diaries*, by Nicole Johns, in which the author chronicles her experience in rehab in a unique way, showcasing journal entries, food plans, and discharge papers through many short chapters. Another is *Sweet Charlotte's Seventh Mistake*, by Cori Crooks, a four-color memoir in photos that is short on words and boundless in its creative expression. You can always set out thinking you're going to write one type of structure and change your mind later, but it's going to be easier on you to commit, try to do a bit of scaffolding, and determine whether you can see the metaview of your memoir from the start, even if the particulars change along the way.

. . . .

What Is a Flashback?

A flashback is an entire scene set in a time that's different from the "current" narrative time of your story—it's not just a memory; it is a full, self-contained scene.

Because of this distinction, flashback is a little trickier than memory. It requires you to be in the scene, to think like your five-year-old, ten-year-old, twenty-year-old self. And because you're transporting yourself back in time, you don't really get to have the insight of the adult, "today" narrator in flashback, whereas with memories you get to say what happened and also comment on it from a more mature place of understanding. But what flashback allows you to do is dive into memory completely, immerse yourself in that time and place, and take your reader fully into that past world as well. It's especially useful when there's an experience or a time in your life that you want to explore more deeply or bring to life more vividly. Then, once you're finished, you can reemerge out of it and continue your story where you left off.

. . . .

OUTLINING (AKA SCAFFOLDING)

Framing and outlining go hand in hand; they're both structural elements. Framing gives you a basic structure for what your memoir is going to be, while outlining fleshes it out—kind of like putting the meat on the bones of your story. Unfortunately, the word "outline" triggers a lot of people. But before you start having nightmares about those outlines your seventh-grade English teacher hammered into your head—those restrictive lists full of Roman numerals and bullet points—let's be clear: that is not what we're talking about.

When we talk about outlining, we want to see something that looks more like Cliffs Notes than like an A, B, C, D, E, F, G type of outline. We encourage you to create narrative summaries of your chapters, rather than bullet-pointed lists. And because this is so different from middle-school English (and because about 80 percent of the people we work with have a knee-jerk reaction to the word "outline"), we like to refer to this kind of mapping with a term Brooke came up with: "scaffolding." With scaffolding, you're creating narrative summaries of each chapter, to the point that anyone who reads them will feel that they are experiencing the story. This reader won't get all the details of your book from these summaries, of course, but they will be able to see the arc of the narrative and have a good sense of the shape and message of each chapter.

Scaffolding is a perfect metaphor for what we're discussing here, because just as you need to have scaffolding in order to build a tower, you need to have scaffolding in order to build your memoir. It's not a permanent, static structure; it's a fluid, supportive entity that moves with you. So, for example, if you're in the middle of your Chapter 2 and you look at your outline for Chapter 3 and realize, *Wow, this is not where I'm going anymore*, that's fine. You just change how you want to focus Chapter 3 at that point. So your memoir scaffolding, just like real scaffolding, is modifiable. If you find that your scaffolding is a little weak or needs to be tweaked in some way, you can just get out your tools and fix it.

For a lot of writers, the idea of outlining is a turnoff because they can't wrap their mind around the entirety of the story and they're overwhelmed by the prospect of it. And feeling overwhelmed, of course, leads to paralysis. We understand that well. But what we've discovered is that most people who are stuck in their memoir are really just begging for structure and are in need of permission to start mapping out their story—with the understanding that it can change later. That's why scaffolding is so great: it's about building out your memoir just a little bit at a time. Instead of outlining all twenty chapters of your memoir *right now*—which probably feels impossible and overwhelming—you can start by outlining the early bits and pieces, maybe just the first couple of chapters to begin with. Then your scaffolding can grow up with you as the chapters are written.

If you are so inclined, your scaffolding can go one step further than figuring out what your chapters will be about. It can detail what the specific scenes within your chapters will be. Again, this doesn't have to be very technical or limiting; you can simply write, "This is what happens in this scene, this is what happens in the next scene," etc. And remember, your outline goes both ways. It's not just a road map to your destination; it's also evidence of where you've been—something to refer back to when you're in Chapter 4, Chapter 5, etc., when you're writing out a scene that's a follow-up to something that you wrote about earlier in your book. Using your scaffolding as your guide makes it easy to look back at Chapter 1 in a moment when you need a reminder of what's been covered and think, *Right—this is where I was then, and this is how that affects this scene.* The more you can use your scaffolding to help you remember where you've already been, the more it will help you as you move forward.

We have noticed that a lot of people, a lot of creatives especially, believe that they should just be able to dive into their writing and have it immediately start to flow. But the thing is, it doesn't always flow, and when you're driving without a map, there's a temptation just to pull over and abandon the car when it gets stuck. We've found that the creative force needs a certain amount of room, but it also needs a certain amount of discipline—something to help us focus and push past what gets in the way—which is why scaffolding is a solution. It's a way to stop and reassess and map your next point when you do get stuck, rather than abandoning the car altogether. Using this approach doesn't mean that you have to be superstrict or stop your creative juices from flowing; it's really about getting support and being able to make it through to the end. That's a freeing feeling—and it can even be fun.

. . . .

Sample Scaffolding

Because we know that people love a template, here's a simple sample scaffolding to help you see both how simple it is—and how helpful—to break down your chapters into scenes that give shape to the arc of your story. Remember, your scaffolding can change as you go. This particular author just scaffolded out one chapter at a time, all the way through to completion.

CHAPTER 1: Horses Coming Back into My Life via Amy (My Middle Daughter)

Scene 1: Walking into barn with 10-year-old Amy to start her proper lessons, introduce her, have exchange/connection with her

Scene 2: Give my context, that I am a mother of three; describe other kids, myself

Scene 3: Flashback: running my horse as 15-year-old, free of rules that ruled my home life

Scene 4: Show the pang of loss—how I was passionate about horses and how I got lost

CHAPTER 2: **Unreachable Mothers/Daughters**

Scene 1: Flashback: pony I had when I was young; my mother late picking me up at the barn

Scene 2: My nanny leaving

Scene 3: Family dynamic, parents, brothers—feeling unloved—fight scene with one of my brothers, he trying to keep me safe, parent me

Scene 4: Fight with Amy—her volatility and need for love—did I fail?

CHAPTER 3: **Animals and Love**

Scene 1: My house as CITY ZOO as a kid—my mother showing me love through animals, and also not being able to show me love as a mother

Scene 2: Flashback: me jumping my dog as a kid—getting my mother's attention—positive and negative

Scene 3: Amy jumping dogs—getting my attention in positive way

Scene 4: Melanie showing me how to parent Amy, to love her

CHAPTER 4: **Riding Again**

Scene 1: Reclaiming horses for myself after watching Amy and my younger daughter, Melanie, for five years. Wanted my own horse. Wanted, needed that connection to sustain me during difficult period with Amy, with my husband.

Scene 2: Telling our trainer I was ready to start riding, having two lessons, then flying to California to try horses to buy

Scene 3: Trying horses, finding a horse, connection with her

Scene 4: Horse show—Amy watching my class—I fall off

CHAPTER 5: Celebrating the Female

Scene 1: Not having beauty/femininity connection with my mother

Scene 2: Buying makeup for Amy with all three kids, broke pattern

Scene 3: Flashback to childhood, my brother making fun of my new bra in front of friends

Scene 4: Amy buying Winter Ball dress, riding bareback

CHAPTER 6: Boundaries

Scene 1: Family dinner with my parents, Amy's 15th bday; Dad makes comment about Amy getting boobs

Scene 2: Phone call to my dad, telling him he cannot speak to girls like that

Scene 3: Therapy session, learning how to set boundaries late in life, becoming educated on what is OK and what is not

Scene 4: Leaving voice mail on brother's machine—I've made a decision not to allow Amy to go on a trip with him and why

Scene 5: Explaining to my dad why I didn't want Amy to go—I was setting boundaries he should have when I was young

CHAPTER 7: **Power in the Alpha Female**

Scene 1: Aftershocks from Ch 6, reflective; putting Amy first allowed me to put myself first with my family; turned to barn and horses again for comfort

Scene 2: Horse show in California, describing different divisions of sport and what our trainer Francesca wants for Amy; Amy tries a new horse

Scene 3: Our trainer is an alpha female. This chapter shows why I'm drawn to her, why I let her make decisions for Amy, saying goodbye to Amy's first horse, bringing a new horse up for trial

Scene 4: Sending Amy to a horse clinic; our trainer helping Amy, helping me by suggesting my horse for Amy, and perhaps a new horse for me

CHAPTER 8: **Transitions**

Scene 1: The new horse in Florida

Scene 2: Selling our old horse; my grief at losing her, feeling pressure from our trainer to buy a new horse; pressure from my husband not to

Scene 3: Amy having a fit in Florida, having to change horses again, feeling my stress

Scene 4: My husband is offered job in New York; we connect in the old way

Scene 5: We tell the kids, Amy thrilled, the other two sad

Scene 6: Conversation with my mother, she knew it was goodbye in profound way, that I would never return

CHAPTER 9: Moving

Scene 1: Melanie playing in boxes, visual mess echoes my internal chaos, my son graduates

Scene 2: Amy sleeps alone in empty house with the cat night before we leave, reality of moving setting in

Scene 3: Horse show goodbyes, Amy's friends, my friends and community who helped me raise Amy, who supported me

Scene 4: On the way to NY, Melanie dislocates her knee, mirroring dislocation of family

Scene 5: Flying east, tale of how we got our animals out to NY

CHAPTER 10: Cultural Anthropology

Scene 1: Horses at new barn. New trainers for us. New trainer for Amy; he's compassionate—contrast with our old trainer.

Scene 2: Seeing the skyline of Manhattan, feeling an energetic cord, hope

Scene 3: Loneliness—missing my son, turning toward my horse for comfort

Scene 4: Amy tutors/SATs, college trip through South, riding in Florida

Scene 5: My son comes to visit, his fight with Amy

CHAPTER 11: **The Launching Years**

Scene 1: Our real estate agent, also a horsewoman, adopts me—maternal figure—perspective on Amy—on surviving brutal childhood positively, compared with my parents

Scene 2: My parents visit, Mom packs Melanie's room, we move to another rental

Scene 3: Move Amy to my trainer Heather, give her my horse

Scene 4: Hurricane Sandy in October, scene huddled in den around fire, girls in hotel

Scene 5: College apps in SV, Florida, Amy's senior pics, watching her ride her new horse/my old horse in the international ring

Scene 6: Amy's graduation, my son's short visit, preparing to move again

Scenes to consider:

- Family of origin scenes; coming back to my family
- Pet scenes

CHAPTER 12: **Home**

Scene 1: After looking at so many houses, finally finding the right one, crying in relief. Family dynamics; exploration of certain tensions.

Scene 2: My husband takes Amy to Italy. I leave and cry at new house, angry at my husband for abandoning me again in a stressful situation but really upset that Amy is leaving for college.

Scene 3: We take Amy to college, the perfect fit for her, why riding so important for her in my opinion. Include a flashback. Driving away with my husband and him saying, "Well, that was easy." Being funny.

Epilogue: I get my horse back (the one I'd originally given to Amy); it's bittersweet. Amy is HAPPY.

. . . .

DEALING WITH YOUR CRITICS

The problem with buckling down and starting to take your writing a little more seriously is that it can encourage the voice of the critic—outer and inner—to start piping up. Both types of critics, especially those we've lived with for a long time and have trouble being objective about, can be crippling if we allow them to be.

The outer critic is anyone who doesn't want you to tell your story or has discouraged you from writing at all. They are often voices from earlier in your life—teachers who told you that your writing wasn't good, for example—or they can be more current voices, like family members who don't want you writing about them. Essentially, anyone in your life who is sending you (or has sent you) messages that somehow sabotage your writing is an outer critic who needs to be silenced.

Then there are inner critics, and these come in many different shades. Some people have a mean, harsh inner critic;

others have a milder one that tells them that they're tired, they've been working too hard, they should rest, they don't need to write right now. There are a million different ways in which these voices emerge and do their best to convince you not to write or tell you that anything you have written is not good enough.

What we have found, having worked with so many authors over the years, is that the best thing you can do with your inner critic is to turn around and face it. If it's a mild voice, sometimes you can just tell it to leave you alone. But for those more forceful voices, the more we run or try to ignore them or push them aside, the stronger they get. To begin working with the critic, write down what the critical voice is saying. This exercise makes you face head-on the critical messages your critic (or critics) is shouting at you. You may even want to write down what it's saying right in the middle of the piece you're working on, because that can give you a clue as to what that voice in your head is getting upset about. First, what is it saying? Second, what is it trying to cover up or hide?

Once you've written down what your inner critic is saying, you can respond to it. Let's say it's telling you that you can't write. Answer it. You could say, for instance, "Well, I can't write as well as I'd like, but I'm in a class and I'm learning and I actually did do pretty well in English, so leave me alone." And then just keep on writing.

The outer critics are tricky in a different way than the inner critics, since the voices may come from the people in your life who are looming large and disrupting your process. Many memoirists have had the experience of someone in their family telling them, "Don't you dare write a memoir." That's a scary thing to hear (or even to imagine hearing). But if you're going to write your story, you need to acknowledge what the voice is saying and claim your space despite your fears. Remind yourself that you have a right to write your story. Remember that you're writing a first draft and you don't need to show it to anyone right now. Right now you're writing your truth, and no one else gets to have a say about that.

GIVING YOURSELF PERMISSION

Confronting and silencing our inner and outer critics is one big way in which we need to release ourselves so we can write. Another is to give ourselves permission to adapt flexibility in our writing—to know that we are allowed to write about whatever we want to, and that we can do so in whatever order makes sense to us.

If you were having a conversation with someone and they asked you about your childhood, you might say, "Oh yeah, this one time when I was growing up, I remember vividly that my dad got really angry at me and it was a really scary moment for me." Then you might follow that up with, "You know, that experience really had an impact on how I interact with people: it made me wary of confrontation." You can see how fluid that was; you looked back at the past, and then you came back to the present and made the connection between what happened before and how you are now. This isn't a big deal—we do it all the time in conversation without even thinking about it—but a lot of writers get really locked into the mindset that they have to follow a chronological timeline, and that makes telling their story harder than it needs to be.

Another thing we need to give ourselves permission to do is to talk about the very private things that have happened in our lives. In society there's an invisible ring around what's okay to talk about and what ways it's okay to be and know and feel. Even if nobody's watching you or reading your writing, writing about personal things can make you feel like you're taking your clothes off and walking around in front of a crowd of strangers. Because of this, memoir is the scariest form of book writing there is—it's very exposing, and it requires you to be vulnerable. You're putting yourself out there, and you're risking a lot. While this is one of the challenges of memoir, it's also the gift that memoir offers you. Think about when you read somebody else's memoir: Aren't you grateful that they were willing to share private moments that are hardly ever talked about? Isn't that what you appreciate most about their story? The truth is, human beings need and want to know how other people are living, how they sort out life and death and loss and joy and discovery and tragedy and everything in between. As hard as it can be to open up in this way, it's also a wonderful thing you're doing when you share your story with the world.

Writing memoir can also be healing. Numerous studies

have shown that writing the truth has a lot of healing power, not only emotionally but physically as well. Most of us know this intuitively—that writing is freeing, that it helps us make sense of the experiences we've had. That's why so many of us like to write in a journal. When you write a memoir, you take freewriting and musing about your life and mold it into a form you can share with others. This process will change you. By the end of writing, revising, and editing your memoir, you will likely have written your way through shame and guilt about what you are revealing in your story. There may be a healing and transformational process for you as you write and revisit your life. By the time your book is published, you will hopefully feel the strength of standing in your truth. After all, it's empowering to shape the story of your life and offer it to others.

Everything that we're saying here is about finding ways to support yourself. You need as much support as you can get, because when you want to start writing your memoir, you may find that a number of things push you away from it. Even when you feel strongly about writing your book, it's still scary, and fear is a great paralyzer. When you can just give yourself permission to begin, to find your voice, to sketch out your ideas and themes, you'll find that the farther along you go, the easier it will become.

HOW TO START WRITING YOUR CHAPTERS

Giving yourself permission to write is one thing; beginning to write is quite another! So where do you actually start when it's time to write your chapters? *How* do you start?

This varies from person to person, and it depends on how structured a person you are. We have found that for many writers, simply creating empty Word documents and labeling them as chapters can be a very motivational exercise. Brooke did this with her first book, *What's Your Book?* While that was a how-to book and not a memoir, we've seen it be an effective approach for memoirists. For instance, if you have your outline and you know that you're going to have ten chapters (for now, anyway—maybe that will change down the road, and that's okay), you can start by creating ten empty Word documents and labeling them as Chapter One.docx, Chapter Two. docx, etc. Then you create a folder on your desktop titled with your memoir title (whatever you're calling it for now). Now you have ten working Word documents that someday will be complete chapters that, together, will be a complete book.

The primary value in doing this exercise is that it can be amazingly inspiring. Every time you open up your memoir folder, you can see all your chapters sitting there—they're unwritten, of course, but they're there waiting for you. They are inviting you. You can sort of see a curled little finger enticing you: *Come on, write me, write me.* It's a great motivator.

This exercise is also valuable in terms of organization. We're not believers in writing your entire memoir in one long Word document. That's going to be fine for the first few chapters, but by the time you get to Chapter 4 and you have eighty or more pages of text, it's going to become overwhelming. Most of you are going to be writing something that is 80,000 words or longer, and that's a lot of words. You don't want to tackle that in a random, "Here I go—I'm going to write a whole book in one go" kind of way. Our minds like to compartmentalize things. So the best way to do it—the only way to do it, we would argue—is one chapter at a time.

This is a huge shift for a lot of writers, because they go from this space of "I'm writing *something*" to "I'm writing *chapters*." It's empowering and solidifies your project. If you've already written a lot of material—if you're drowning in notes, partial drafts, half-written chapters—this kind of organization gives you a way to move things into their appropriate places, and to start separating things out. If you don't want to clutter your chapter files with random bits and pieces, you can take this a step further and for each chapter create a "dump" file (Chapter 1 Dump.docx, Chapter 2 Dump.docx—be sure to label them clearly), which is a document where you keep those extra ideas and scenes that don't quite yet have a home in the chapter, passages you love but that don't fit the scaffolding as you move forward.

Once you start creating all these files, you'll want to attend to housekeeping on your computer on a regular basis, too. It's essential to clearly name *and* date every file you create. That way, even if you end up writing ten different drafts of Chapter

1, you'll always be able to find the most recent version. This is especially vital for those writers who have been working on their book for years; it's easy to lose track of what's what when that much time has passed since you started. Dating your files is a simple way to avoid the headache (and heartache) of misplacing, or even accidently overwriting or deleting, pieces of writing you've put so much work into.

The hard truth is, no matter how much writing and processing you've done—pages and pages of freewriting, a lot of "shitty first drafts," as Anne Lamott calls them—you're eventually going to get to a place where you need a system of some kind. So many people we've worked with have come to us because they've written 100,000 words but the text is a mess. Even after all the time they've put in, they still don't have a book. If this is where you are, you're probably feeling very overwhelmed. But take it from us: there is a way out of this stuck-ness, and a large part of it has to do with getting organized and doing an inventory of what you have. You need to dust and sweep so that you can sit down and have some clear space—even if you have a ton of content already and you know it's going to take a long time to do it. However time-consuming it might be, we can guarantee you that if you keep going without making an effort to organize, finishing your book is going to take far longer.

The same goes for you if you're just starting to work on your memoir. Do yourself a huge favor and implement these strategies now. It's a little bit like attending to your bills: it's not glamorous and it's not fun, but taking care of it lifts a great weight from your mind. When you don't have this mess and this clutter taking up your mental space, you will feel freer to dive in and approach your writing in a more conscious, more present way.

. . . .

Have a Lot of Content Already? Take Inventory!

There are three primary ways to organize your ideas and content when you are getting started in earnest with your memoir. If you already have a lot of content written, you want to start with an inventory of what you already have. This helps you take stock of your existing material. What you have might be entire chapters, or just scenes. When you do an inventory of what you have, you want to use narrative summary, similar to the scaffolding idea—CliffsNotes-style. Then list the word count of that particular piece of writing underneath the summary. Limit your summary to a maximum of three or four sentences, as part of your discipline. You don't want to have long, drawn-out summaries. They exist just as reminders of what content you have, for the purpose of integrating it all into your scaffolding at a later point.

. . . .

FREEWRITING

We've mentioned freewriting several times now, but we haven't really discussed what it is or how it can benefit you. So let's jump in and talk about that for a moment.

Freewriting is exactly what it sounds like: a practice that allows you to write freely, without holding anything back. You're not taking your time to select your words carefully; you're writing fast. It's a brain dump—a "download," as our colleague Jennifer Lauck calls it—of ideas and beginnings, anything that pops into your head. One of the great things about writing fast like this is that you end up blowing by a lot of those critical voices that have been holding you back.

Various authors have written about freewriting—Julia Cameron's *The Artist's Way* and Dorothea Brande's *Becoming a Writer* come to mind—and their directions are all pretty much the same: You put your pen on the page (or your fingers on the keyboard), and you write whatever comes out. Don't censor, don't delete, don't cross out—just write whatever comes out for fifteen or twenty minutes. We think the ideal is twenty minutes. That may sound tough to do, but once you get started, you'll find that the time goes by in a flash.

Of course, if you want to keep going after those twenty minutes, you can, but you may not find it necessary. Even within that short time, things will show up on that page that will be unexpected little gifts. We've been talking a lot about various structured ways to get started, but if you're really stuck, freewriting can help you shake things up and begin to get some words on the page. The more you do this, the more you'll discover: you'll find out things that you didn't know you were going to say; you'll uncover ideas and thoughts you didn't know you had; and you'll claim your voice.

If you're extremely right-brained and you can't get your mind around an outline, freewriting probably appeals to you a lot. Some people just need to write, write, write so they can figure out what they're trying to say or simply get it out of their body—and if that's the case for you, that's okay. This is where your turning points will come in handy, because they can help prevent you from getting lost in the mess. You need to be free to write what you need to write, but you don't want to stray too far from the path. So try picking a turning point—one that's really calling out to you—and freewrite around that. You'll still have the freedom of writing fast and not censoring yourself, but you'll also be focusing on something that you know you want to include in your book.

Many of us simply need permission to be able to do the messy work. Our feeling is that freewriting can be hugely valuable—but you have to know whether it's serving you or not. If you're doing it from an intentional space of "I know I just have to push through this; otherwise I'm not going to write it," that's perfectly fine. But if you're doing it from an unfocused, random place, or if you've been toiling away for five or six years on this thing and you're still in the "shitty first draft," then you need to try to approach your writing from a more structured place.

That said, there is a magic around just writing. Not all of what comes out when you freewrite will necessarily be worth publishing, but that doesn't mean it's not valuable. If nothing else, the act of writing, in and of itself, leads to more writing. Frequently what will happen is you'll start freewriting and all of a sudden a story will appear to you and you'll go, *Oh my gosh, I've got to write this story!* When that fire-in-the-belly moment happens, *use* it—see where it takes you. You don't have to be single-mindedly methodical at every moment; you can let your creative juices take over once in a while.

MAKING TIME FOR YOUR WRITING

Wherever you are in your process—whether you're in the left-brained space of working on your outline, or letting your right brain take over for a while and freewriting—you're not going to get very far if you don't make time for your writing.

Most of us have busy lives, and that can make it hard to prioritize our writing time. There are various methods, if you're one of those people who can't seem to find the time to write, that you can use to get your writing done.

One approach is to make a writing date with yourself—to take your computer or just your paper and pen, get out of your house, and go to a café or a pub. Once you're there, you'll want to turn off your email and all the other stuff that can come flowing in, set a certain amount of time for yourself to write, and really focus. If the noise of a public place is distracting for you, wear headphones. The important thing is to get out of your house. Maybe you have a young child or a partner, or perhaps you're just not good at focusing when you could be doing other things (cleaning, watching TV, making dinner, etc.). Whatever your reasons, if you're not good at getting your writing done at home, it's critical to understand that about yourself and find a space that works for you.

You can also make writing dates with writer friends. It's easiest to break our appointments with ourselves, so bringing another person into the equation can make a huge difference. And this kind of date doesn't even have to be in person—you can simply have a writing buddy whom you make goals with and check in with each week via phone or email. If you need more accountability, you can go one step further and agree that each of you will email the other every time you sit down to work on your project—"I'm here, I'm writing"—and then email them again when you're done. We think of this as a sort of "writers' gym." It's like having your own personal-training buddy who's making you at least show up.

All of this creates the mindset that you're a writer—that you're working on your book, taking it seriously, setting aside time for it, and making it a priority in your life. It tells your subconscious, "I'm in this; now come on—help me out." This is important, because your unconscious mind wants to flake out or procrastinate by watching TV, and it's easy to succumb to this desire. There will be a lot of days when you simply won't want to write. But you'll find that over time, bailing on your writing—failing to honor your writer self—will begin to weigh on you. Writers feel much better when they're writing.

EMBRACING STRUCTURE

The things we've discussed in this chapter will help you do more than just write a book; they'll help you create a writing life. As you're discovering, writing a memoir is more than simply sitting down and writing. All this planning and structuring helps you create an all-encompassing support system—one that will hold you, your project, and your process and help you stay on track from start to finish.

Writing, of course, is an art, so there's no one right process for any single person, but we have seen over and over again with the many clients and students we've worked with that having some sense of this road map we've been talking about is freeing. We know that many people think, *Oh my God, I'm going to be beholden to this outline, and it's going to dampen everything about my creative process*. But what your scaffolding really does is allow you to have a sense of where you're going and to funnel your creative energy into something productive, rather than feeling panicked and lost and overwhelmed. So even if you think this whole outlining thing isn't for you, at least give yourself permission to take a weekend—it probably won't take more than a few hours—at least to do an inventory of what you've done so far and organize what you have.

Many poets talk about how creatively liberating it is for them to have to write a sestina, a villanelle, something with a highly structured form. They say that having some boundaries helps them break into a deeper level of creativity. The same freedom goes for memoirists. These skills will help you forever—with this memoir, and with your next memoir, and with anything else you write in the future.

CHAPTER 3:

The Art of Storytelling

In his book *Self Comes to Mind*, neuroscientist Antonio Damasio writes the following about storytelling and the brain: "Implicit storytelling has created our selves, and it should be no surprise that it pervades the entire fabric of human societies and cultures."

We couldn't agree more. Storytelling is how we make sense of the world around us; the brain is always seeking meaning from all the different input it's receiving, and the narrative form gives us a way not only to synthesize that meaning but also to share it with others. Story, to paraphrase author Lisa Cron in her wonderful book, *Wired for Story*, is the language of experience. We all have it within us.

That doesn't mean, of course, that masterful storytelling is easy. As we've seen in Chapters 1 and 2 of this book, a lot goes into even *preparing* to write a memoir, let alone actually doing the writing. And if you're a more right-brained writer, all this planning and outlining probably feels a bit overwhelming. So let's take a step back. In this chapter, we'll look at the big picture—the narrative arc, themes, takeaways, and how you can use your right brain as a tool to further your story. This information will help even the most dedicated fly-by-the-seat-of-their-pants writers stay focused on what's important in their memoir. So let's get started!

NARRATIVE ARC

There are many different story structures in the world, as we mentioned in Chapter 2. But the classic narrative arc is one that's often used in screenwriting: the three-act structure. If you watch a lot of movies, you're probably familiar with this. Act One sets up the story: it introduces the characters and situations and provides the context for everything that follows. In a movie, the first twenty minutes covers most of these setups. Sometimes the camera starts out far away and zooms in on a town and then a house and the people in the house, and then focuses on what one of those people is doing or saying. In those first few minutes, barely into the story, you're trying to understand what's happening. The who, what, where, when, and why are being laid out before you. We wonder, who are these people, what are they doing, where are they, when is their story taking place, and why are we watching them right now? Then Act Two gets to the meat of the story and Act Three offers some sort of resolution.

In fiction from the nineteenth century—like Dickens, for instance—you would notice a lot of lecturing to the audience at the beginning of a story, long passages of exposition and explanations, but that's not generally the custom now. Most stories today start *in medias res*—in the middle of things. In memoir, then, you want to think about starting with something that kicks off your primary theme or immediately shows the reader why you're telling your story. You build up layers of complexity that lead up to the second act, including—and this is very important—setting up the reader to identify with the protagonist, who in memoir, of course, is *you*. You are the narrator, and you are the main character. The reader needs to be on board with you as you play these dual roles in your memoir.

John Lanchester does a wonderful job of helping the reader understand his role as the narrator and protagonist in his memoir, *A Family Romance*. He makes it clear right away that his book is an identity quest, posing questions like, "Who was my mother, really?" "Who were my father and grandparents?" "What is the truth of where I came from?" Because he sets us up properly early in the book, by the time he starts digging down into the past, finding photographs and piecing together his family's history, we're completely with him. We feel led to all the layers of his richly characterized story about both sets of grandparents and his own parents, as well as his own place in their stories. He hooks us in the first act, and we're happy to go along for the ride.

Linda Joy's memoir, *Don't Call Me Mother*, also begins right in the middle of things—she starts with her mother leaving her at the train station—but that isn't how she initially began her story; in fact, that's not how she started any of her first ten drafts. Ultimately, she realized that this moment—being abandoned, watching her mother leave—was the beginning of her primary theme. Setting it up at the beginning allowed her to lay the groundwork for everything that followed. That is what you should be looking for: the entry point that will simultaneously draw the reader in and give them the context they need to understand everything that follows.

So now we come to Act Two, the middle of the book, which is where the plot—the events that unfold in your book—develops more complexity. If you're writing a memoir, you're writing it because one or several significant issues have appeared in your life and you're trying to write your way through them; you want to write your memoir so you can figure them out. Act Two is where you're going to delve into what happened and how you reacted to these challenges. What were the complications, the surprises, and the conflicts you encountered?

You may be one of those people who don't like the word "conflict." Let's be clear: conflict doesn't need to be dish throwing or car chases or fistfights. In this context, conflict is any struggle for power or voice, no matter how big or small. It can be as simple as someone telling you when you were a child to go clean your room and you responding, "I don't want to; can't I just play for five more minutes?" That's conflict. (We'll discuss this in more detail in Chapter 4, when we talk about scenes.)

Essentially, this middle part of the book is where you're struggling with what your themes are, the essence of your story, and what you need to say. You're trying to figure out what you're going to do to write yourself into the core messages of your story, to get to the heart of how it needs to unfold.

Then we come to the last act, Act Three, which is where you may find the beginning of some sort of resolution for you, the narrator, and for some of the characters in your story. (And by characters, of course, we mean people in your life.) At this point in the book, the questions that you have been wrestling with are answered, or at least brought to as much resolution as is possible. This is memoir, after all, not fiction, and real life doesn't usually get ironed out as neatly as we might like. But regardless of whether you have everything figured out by the end or not, the reader should understand what they're supposed to be taking away from your story when they're done with your book. They should be thinking, *I get it. This is what this person was trying to figure out. This is where they are now.*

Again, you don't have to tie your story off with a bow; it's entirely possible to end a memoir and leave the reader with a lot of satisfaction even if you don't have a clear-cut way to wrap things up. Naturally, it can be difficult to figure out how to do this; how do you end a story that doesn't have an end? It's a question that many authors come up against, and unfortunately there's no one right answer. Knowing what your themes are and how you're handling them, however, is a great way to help yourself get there. As you write yourself toward the end, the creative process will help guide you to where you need to be.

. . . .

What's Really Worth Including?

Here, we're talking about getting to the resolution of your story, and let's just preface this by saying that it's different for everyone. In some memoirs, most of the story is about the problem, and then—boom—maybe somebody apologizes or somebody dies or some other momentous event occurs, but whatever it is, it brings about a relatively speedy resolution. In others, the resolution comes about more slowly. Regardless of how it happened in "real life," whether or not your narrative arc works is a matter of balance and pacing.

If you're worried about whether you're doing a good job of moving your plot forward, you need to ask yourself if the scenes you have included are driving the story onward, or if you're just showcasing the various problems you have encountered along the way. We see a lot of memoirists getting caught in a net of problems.

While it's true that people have crazy stories, lives where they have faced and overcome one problem after another, and they want to show how they came through it, it's important to make sure your memoir doesn't end up feeling like a play-by-play of a disastrous life: "Here's all the horrible stuff that happened, and then here's some more horrible stuff." It's difficult to know how to handle the truth of your life when you've faced multiple hardships, and we want to support you in sorting this out. People do suffer multiple catastrophic events and losses, and of course you want to include what happened and be honest about the problems you faced, but the reader is looking for some kind of redemption, so you have to offer glimmers of that redemption throughout your story. You can't just say, "And this happened and then that happened and then this happened," because your readers won't stick around if that's all you're giving them. There have to be more layers of self-understanding and transformation than that.

What we would suggest, if you're having difficulty distinguishing between what's important to include in your story and what is simply gratuitous, is that you look to memoirists who have handled this question well—to read other people who have a firm grasp on that balance. Examples of memoirs we love that have chosen their details and arc well include *Jesus Land,* by Julia Scheeres, and *The Glass Castle.* These are both coming-of-age memoirs in which the authors face troubling situations in their upbringing yet manage to show these situations dispassionately and without judgment, so that the reader can interpret what they will in reading the work. The classic memoir *This Boy's Life,* by Tobias Wolff, focuses on a certain time in his adolescence—a slice of his life during a time that's rife with abandonment, domestic violence, and delinquency—and yet he doesn't overdo it; he shows us just enough to keep us hooked. Frank McCourt, in *Angela's Ashes,* paints his "miserable Irish childhood," as he puts it, in living color—with scents, sounds, description, and dialogue that take us fully into his world—but keeps a balance of detail, emotion, and pacing.

Reading others' work can help you see how far the writer has dived into the physical, emotional, and mental aspects of their experiences, revealing enough to involve you as a reader, but not enough to overwhelm you. Read memoirs first for pleasure and later for how much they shared and what's implied in their layers of description, dialogue, and detail. Ask yourself if you feel there's too much or just enough. Then go back to your own work and ask yourself, *Is all this detail too much? Am I getting sick of these stories? Am I getting bored with myself? Or do I need to show these details to paint the picture clearly? Did I offer a takeaway or universal message for the reader?*

For some writers, this is the point at which you'll want to hire someone to do an assessment of your manuscript. When you're too close to a story, it can be hard to know whether it's good or not. If this is where you are—if you feel like you don't have any sense of whether your story is boring, or if you feel like something's not quite right but you can't put your finger on why—it can be helpful for you to get a professional read. You'll be amazed at what a little outside perspective can bring to your story.

. . . .

THEMES

Writing a memoir without themes in mind is like turning on a hose without putting a bucket underneath it: all the water pours out haphazardly and flows away from you, seeping into the ground. Your themes are containers; they keep your writing together. When you can identify them and weave them throughout your memoir, you answer the questions of what it is that you're writing and what it is that you want the reader to experience.

An autobiography doesn't have to be thematic; it just leads readers through each event in the author's life. But memoir does have to be thematic in order for it to be what we've been describing: a slice of life—something that can be categorized and shelved as a memoir within a particular category, like coming-of-age, travel, transformation, or addiction. In some cases, your category will also be your theme. That is frequently the case in terms of life events—the death of a loved one, for instance. Take Joan Didion's *The Year of Magical Thinking*, a book that's about the author's life after her husband's death, about living through grief. Bereavement is a category of memoir, but it is also a theme and an emotion. So sometimes these two things, category and theme, cross-populate. Not always—but sometimes.

Sticking to your themes doesn't mean that your memoir has to be as structured as a book like *Eat, Pray, Love*, where Elizabeth Gilbert splits the narrative by where she is (Italy, India, Indonesia) and what she's doing there (eating, praying, loving). This is an example of the most structured, thematic memoir you can have, and yes, it works quite well—but then you have others that are very loose but still very compelling. Take Anne Lamott's memoirs. She does write very thematically, and her categories are always clean and delineated. One book is about motherhood, and another one is about grandparenthood. Several books are about spirituality. But within those containers, she jumps around quite a bit. And ultimately that works because after reading one of her books, the reader walks away feeling touched by what they've read. Lamott achieves this effect because even though she doesn't always follow a linear path, she never loses sight of her theme (or themes, as the case may be).

The concept of writing thematically can be confusing, so

let's get a little more specific and choose an emotion you could use as a theme. Let's say it's love. So, imagine: You are totally in love. You've never felt this way before; you're on cloud nine. Everyone knows what that feels like and how it colors your view of the world. In this case, love is the impulse or the thing that is driving you through your memoir. You are in that space where you're feeling those feelings of being in love, and that comes through in every line of your writing. This is writing memoir through what Brooke calls "theme-colored glasses." The idea here is that everything you write should be tinged with your theme. You must remember to put on those glasses before you write, to help you stay focused and to view the world you're writing about through a particular lens. In this example, the emotion of love is infusing your writing. Therefore the memoir would always be tying back in to love, relationships, the emotional complexities of love, even if the author were experiencing eating a meal out, traveling to another country, or meeting a new friend. With love-tinted lenses on, the author would perceive these experiences as having a particular tone or color, different from that of a memoir whose theme was addiction, for instance.

Of course, by the time you're writing your memoir, you may not be feeling that overwhelming sense of love and obsession anymore. Or you may no longer be an addict, or you may no longer be resentful about your divorce, or you may be past the height of conflict with a family member. Even so, you need to be able to bring all of those emotions to the forefront when you're writing your memoir—you need to be able to write as if you are still walking through life with those lenses on when the story calls for it.

That can be 1) difficult to do, and 2) very painful. If you're writing about something positive, like love or a wonderful year of living abroad, then this probably won't be too difficult for you, but if you're writing about a traumatic upbringing or the ways in which your peers ostracized you when you were a teenager, that's a whole other story. Looking deeply at that theme through a focused lens requires you to relive those times and to reexperience those feelings. When this is the case, you might be tempted not to dig too deeply or to skim over certain things. We completely understand why: this process of remembering and digging and focusing can be very complicated and messy. Themes are essential to your narrative. They can feel like an abstract concept, but themes help you to stay focused and contained. Think of them as the fertile soil underneath your experiences, feeding you and shaping your understanding—and, by extension, your readers' experience—of your world.

. . . .

Can a Conflict or Struggle Be a Theme?

We want to be clear that a theme is not the same thing as a conflict or struggle. Your themes are energies or emotions, the ongoing issues that color your experiences. So if you're writing a memoir about being gay and Christian, for example, religion in and of itself could be a theme, because it's a structure that is imposed upon your life; it's something that you can process. Also, a gay man's experience or a lesbian's experience can be thematic, because, again, that's a lens through which you see the world. It affects how you perceive the things that happen to you. Your theme in a case like this might be overcoming a struggle, or grappling with a heavy experience that's tough to reconcile. The theme can't be the conflict itself of being gay and Christian.

Or let's say your memoir is a coming-of-age story about having a tough time in high school. "Coming of age" is a category, but it's not a theme on its own. The theme resides underneath your story. It's the fuel that feeds your story, the lens through which you see the world. For this high school narrative, it's important to get to the root of why you had such a hard time at this point in your life. What was it that caused these struggles? Did it have anything to do with family dynamics, for example? Family dynamics definitely can be a theme; lots of people have written entire memoirs that are really just about the dynamics of relationships—mother-daughter memoirs, mother-father memoirs, son-father memoirs, etc. Two powerful father-son memoirs are *Beautiful Boy,* by David Sheff, and *Tweak,* by David's son Nic Sheff. These are memoirs about Nic's addiction to meth, so they're both addiction memoirs, though one is told through the father's lens of how the addiction affected the family, while the other, told through the lens of the addict himself, is more insular and self-centered in a sense, but also more about the internal conflict versus the family dynamic conflict.

Your theme is something that has bearing on your worldview, and it's also something that's universal. Everyone knows what it's like to struggle; everyone knows what it's like have a complex relationship with a loved one; everyone understands grief and loss, even if they've not yet experienced it themselves on a profound level. Universal truths are the touch points for themes, by which we mean that if you've hit upon something universally resonant, it's likely that you've discovered a theme.

The struggles and conflicts that take place in your memoir are plot points, not themes. They're the elements that comprise the arc of your story. To get to your themes, you need to dig deeper. Your themes are the foundation under everything. They are the oxygen that infuses the story. Sometimes you can't see it, but there's a subtle thread holding things in place that readers often respond to, even if they don't fully understand why. A brilliant example of this can be seen in a thematic memoir like Elizabeth Gilbert's *Eat, Pray, Love*. Gilbert's memoir was conceived based on three themes: eating in Italy (the theme here was passion); praying in

India (the theme here was devotion); and loving in Indonesia (the theme here was not specifically romantic love, but rather dedication—to self and to others). If you read Gilbert's memoir with this framework in mind, you will see that she holds a very contained environment for exploration of these themes—and we believe this is one of the fundamental reasons this memoir was as popular as it was.

If you're having a difficult time identifying your theme(s), ask yourself, *What were the things that caused my pain and the struggle?* Or, if your story is more about positive experiences that encouraged change in your life, you could ask, *What were the things that inspired my personal growth?* Find the answers to these questions, and you will likely find your themes.

. . . .

TAKEAWAYS

If you look at any of the memoirs that have hit the best-seller lists in the past ten years, they all have a very clear message and takeaway. Sometimes it's simply "I had a crazy experience growing up that I really want to share," as in *Running with Scissors*, by Augusten Burroughs. Sometimes it's "This is how I broke free of my addiction," as was the case with *The Tender Bar*, by J. R. Moehringer. But all successful best-selling memoirs have a takeaway that offers up the specific events and experiences of a person's life as universal truths for the reader to absorb and ultimately relate to. Your memoir needs to do this, too.

For every scene you write in your memoir, you need to ask yourself, *What is the reader learning from this situation?* That is the takeaway. You have to provide these takeaways and pay attention to what we call "universalisms"—experiences that we all share, that we can all relate to, even if our situations aren't identical—if you want to keep the reader interested in your story. If you're not keeping your reader in mind and you're just writing away, you've probably lost sight of what matters about your story to another person, which detracts from your memoir's value and makes your readers lose interest.

As a beginner, you'll find that the best place to plant your takeaways is at the end of your chapters and/or at the end of scenes; they're easy places to wrap something up and get the reader thinking. For example, at the end of a chapter in Jen Larsen's *Stranger Here: How Weight Loss Surgery Transformed My Body and Messed with My Head*, a memoir Brooke worked on while she was at Seal Press, the author provides a takeaway in the form of her reaction to a friend's telling her she looks fantastic:

> "'Thank you,' I said, and I beamed. I didn't say, 'But every time I lose a pound it feels as if I'm taking a step away from a person I used to be.' I am deliber-

ately dissociating myself from the body I had given myself and the life I had led all the way up to my highest weight. I am abandoning the person I was, negating all of my previous accomplishments—my entire life. Debbie was complimenting me on not being that person anymore. I soaked it up."

This is powerful because even if we personally have not lost weight in the way in which the author did, we can still wrap our minds around the idea of dissociating ourselves from our bodies or our lives. This is a takeaway; it invites you to consider times when you've felt high or low, and encourages your mind to make an association with a similar moment or emotion you've experienced in your own life. Note that you don't necessarily have to step away from your story. You don't have to pontificate or philosophize in order to offer a takeaway (although you can if you want to, of course). You just need to consider what it is that you're sharing and talk about it in a way that will allow your reader to connect with it.

You may not know exactly what all of your takeaways will be when you first start out, and that's okay; that's one reason to write your memoir—to make these discoveries about the universalisms of a story that may at first feel very particular and personal to you. Wisdom can pop out at unexpected moments. The trick is to be open to it.

RIGHT-BRAIN EXERCISES
FOR MEMOIRISTS

We've been talking a lot about planning and structure—all very left-brained stuff. But part of staying open to the little wisdoms that will surface as you write your story is keeping the right side of your brain active and stimulated. Freewriting, which we discussed in Chapter 2, is part of this. But there are a number of other things you can do to release your creativity as a memoirist as well. Let's take a closer look at some of them.

Embrace Your Memories

We know that after what happened with *A Million Little Pieces* and James Frey, many memoirists feel nervous about getting things right, as if everything has to be documented. Frey wrote what was basically a fictional account of his story but called it a memoir, and the ramifications have been deep and lasting for many writers because they have tapped into the fear that they have to get every single detail exactly right or they'll get in trouble—perhaps even get sued. As a result, memoirists have become uptight about using their imagination. They get tangled up about the accuracy of their memory, and they start worrying—*Am I remembering this correctly? Should I write it the way everyone else says it happened, or should I write it the way I remember it?*

In a lot of ways, our memories define our identity. Think about what happens when older people get dementia or suffer memory loss: they become lost, and their family does as well, because the ability to remember things had so much to do with who they were as a person. And there are some memories we may be holding on to that everyone else in our life disagrees with. As one of our colleagues, writer Mark Matousek, once said to Linda Joy in an interview, "Memory *is* imagination." It's in your mind; it's nothing tangible. So don't be scared that you're imagining. You can look up the facts later if you want to make sure the scene you're setting is accurate, but when you're creating—when you're in the moment—let 'er rip. Don't censor yourself for fear of not getting every single detail exactly right.

In our classes, we talk about the power of emotional truth. You did not walk through your life with a tape recorder, and therefore you don't have a transcript of all the events of your life exactly as they've unfolded. That said, it's one thing to invent something that did not happen, and quite another thing to write a portrait of an event you lived through based on the facts *as you remember them*. You will often have to embellish scenes with details—what people were wearing and what exactly was spoken—and this is to be expected. It's part of writing a story. It's unfortunate that so many memoirists have outright invented scenes and/or intentionally lied, because it permeates the entire memoir-writing community. We truly believe that your emotional truth should be your barometer of what's okay to write about, and we hope that you'll find comfort and write the truth of your experience as you remember it. Current practices have you put a disclaimer in your book stating that you have written the story as you remember it. This means that you are allowed to create scenes and dialogue, and to take creative license in the writing of them, to offer the essence (and emotional truth) of what happened.

Create a Mind Map

As you go through your memories and start to get your scenes down on paper, you want to ask yourself, *What metaphor, what imagery, or what history does this evoke?* One great tool that can help you with this is called a "mind map."

Mind mapping is very simple. Start this exercise by putting your theme or your topic—let's say it's the loss of your father—in the center of a circle on a piece of paper. Then draw lines off of that central circle and create bubbles at the ends of them, and fill those bubbles with anything you come up with that you associate with that topic—just what you remember and how you associate with that topic. What his hair was like. How he smoked a pipe. The smell of his clothes. Your favorite thing you ever did with him. Your least favorite thing you ever did with him. What happened at his funeral. What happened the day before. What happened the day after. Just keep going until you've exhausted your associations.

You'll end up with this cluster of images, ideas, and moments—and maybe some of them will evoke a spark of interest that's relevant to the theme of your memoir or where you lived or the era you lived in. This could lead you to doing some research after you've gotten most of your story down, or perhaps you'll want to explore some of these branches more deeply, which will provide you with a richness of detail that you can add into your story. Take notes, write more, and come back and paint it in, layer by layer, detail by detail, until you have your final version.

Stop and Listen

Sometimes you need to stop trying so hard and simply pay attention to what your mind is telling you. When Linda Joy was writing her first book, there were times when she wasn't sure what she was going to write in the next chapter—she had an outline, but she felt stuck—so she would put what she had under her pillow and say to herself when she was going to sleep, *Okay, unconscious, please help me tonight. I'm in a hurry to get this thing done, and I need some ideas for this next chapter.* As silly as it may sound, it worked—she would wake up with an idea or with a better understanding of how to finish something she'd already started. Something clicked.

This is why, when people are stuck or struggling, we often tell them to go and sit outside for a while, or look out their window and write what they see, or turn on some music and meditate—anything to trigger their artistic sensibilities, their imagination. Our left brain is always ticking away, so it's vital to get in tune with the right brain once in a while, to be present and listen to what's going on both around and inside you.

BRINGING BOTH SIDES TOGETHER

When it comes down to it, you need both the right and the left brain in order to write a memoir. It's not about cultivating or tending to one over the other; rather, it's about bringing them together to make your story fly. If you happen to be more of a right-brained person, you probably need to bring a bit of structure into your memoir experience. If you happen to be more of a left-brained person, you may need to give yourself permission to explore your creativity by trying something new, even (or especially) if you feel it falls outside your comfort zone. Ultimately, your goal, in addition to creating a beautifully crafted, cohesive memoir, is to stay sane. Writing a memoir requires a lot of you, and the more you can show up wholly and completely, the better the story you'll have to offer to your eventual readers.

CHAPTER 4

Craft

We've used the term "craft" a few times so far in this book—but what *is* craft, exactly? Craft, to us, has to do with using the tools you have in your toolbox to create an experience for the reader—and for yourself—when you're writing. As John Gardner writes in *The Art of Fiction*, "In the writing state—the state of inspiration—the fictive dream springs up fully alive: the writer forgets the words he has written on the page and sees, instead, his characters moving around their rooms, hunting through cupboards, glancing irritably through their mail, setting mousetraps, loading pistols." This quote is technically about fiction writing, but it applies just as aptly to memoir: you are striving to create a seamless world, a dream that will hold the reader within it from page one until your conclusion.

A lot of people we've taught have told us that they've been writing for years and that no one has ever talked to them about craft in the way we talk about it. If this is the case for you, believe us, we understand this might feel frustrating and overwhelming. But once you become aware of the various elements of craft that you have at your disposal, you'll truly start to see your writing take on a level of sophistication and nuance that will thrill you. Once you're aware of the existence of these skills and tools, your access to them is only a matter of developing and deepening them. Remember, no one starts out with a completely comprehensive handle on memoir. It takes practice, and it also takes reading other people's memoirs; as you become a more discerning reader, you will unquestionably become a better writer.

In Chapter 1, we discussed narrative voice, which is one of the major elements of the craft of memoir. In this chapter, we're going to discuss the other two primary elements—scenes and plot—as well as through-threads and the importance of transparency and relatability in memoirs. Together, these tools will help you create a more cohesive and complete memoir.

WRITING SCENES

If you've been writing for a while, you've probably heard a lot about showing versus telling; you may even have heard that you should always show, not tell—a teaching that we believe can become detrimental to your memoir writing. After all, a book that's all "show" and no "tell" is a book that's all action, all dialogue, all about "what happened," and no narrative summary (which drives the plot along) or opportunities for reflection (what we call "takeaway"). Scenes are not, as writers might believe, composed solely of dialogue and action. As we discussed in Chapter 1, scenes are building blocks of your chapters. We like to think of scenes as beads on a necklace that create your chapters. Scenes create a special lived and felt moment in time. You want the reader to feel and know you intimately, to walk in your shoes as the "main character" of your memoir. They are also invitations into the fictive dream, where your responsibility is to show the who, what, when, where, why, and how, and to use as many sensory details as you want to create a world for your readers.

A well-written scene should center on an event that propels the story forward, and in each scene there should be at least some small measure of character development, where the characters—you, other people who are involved in your story—go through some kind of change. As you're writing a scene, you should ask yourself, *Why is this scene here?* If you can't answer that question—if nothing actually happens—then it almost certainly shouldn't be in your book.

Of course, there are always exceptions to the rule. After all, some scenes exist solely to push forward the plot. Other scenes exist for the singular purpose of inviting the reader deeper into the dream you're creating on the page, to get a clearer picture of the experience the writer had, which she's trying to convey to you in a deep and experiential way. In *Wild*, Cheryl Strayed has a scene where she meanders off the Pacific Crest Trail and comes into contact with a young man on a bike. The scene does nothing but showcase her interaction with him. It seems almost meaningless, and you might ask yourself why she chose to include it. But for us it showcases what life was like on the trail, and the contrast of the people hiking the trail, who had a camaraderie around the very fact that they were doing this thing "together," versus those people off the trail, who seemed nearly otherworldly to Strayed.

In scenes that exist to push forward the plot, there may not be much actual character development, and there may not be much action. These scenes are more focused on narrative summary and less on dialogue and tone and body language. Know that there is a place for all of it, and that a scene doesn't look just one way. What defines a scene, again, is simply that it be a contained narrative that's like a movie clip of significant moments chosen from the flow of time that express our experiences as vividly as we can. The details of how something looks, smells, and feels, and how the world imposes itself upon your body and mind, are what the reader is following in your scenes. Remember, the most important thing you can do in the various kinds of scenes you are writing is to bring the reader into your world completely and weave that world so well, your reader doesn't want to leave.

It is important to keep in mind that a scene cannot be just thoughts. Yes, for a protagonist who has some kind of conflict or problem or issue that you're trying to solve, there's likely going to be a lot of reflection, but you can't just write a whole bunch of philosophical things that are going on in your head and leave it at that. This kind of reflection and connection to bigger ideas is important, and might function as part of your reflections on your experiences, but your reflections should not feel like sermons. No matter what you're thinking about in a given scene, you had to be thinking these things somewhere, at a certain time and in a certain place. So locate yourself there: Include the sights and smells and activities swirling around you. Ground your thoughts in that particular moment. Immerse your reader.

In order to write scene well, you should be asking yourself a number of questions as you write, including:

- What is this situation that I'm in?
- What do I want the reader to know?
- What are they learning from this situation?
- What is the action?
- How do the other people in this scene move and talk?
- What language, what tone, do I want to use here?

In *Wired for Story*, Lisa Cron writes about what happens to us physically when we're reading a scene and why we need draw upon specific details when writing a scene. The more sensory detail we write, the more it engages our brain to relive the experience—and this translates to our reader. According to Cron, brain scans have shown that parts of our brain light up when we read about an activity in exactly the same way they light up when we perform that activity, which is why scenes with specific details create a vivid experience for the reader.

When we look at a picture, different landscapes and different portraits make us feel different things. You want to achieve this same sort of visceral evocation in your scenes with descriptions, sounds, smells, textures, and a feeling about the place where your scene is occurring. This is what we're talking about when we say that you need to immerse your reader. If you're sitting near a lake in the evening in one scene, for example, you might write about hearing the crunching of leaves as people walk by, or perhaps a rustling in the trees if the wind is blowing. Maybe it's begun to mist and you write about the damp, heavy feeling of it and the way you take the air into your lungs; you might write about the smell of smoke from a campfire somewhere nearby. All of these things belong in your scene and help to bring the moment to life.

Aside from sensual details, which we will discuss at greater length in Chapter 5, dialogue is a fundamental element—and craft point—of many scenes (not all scenes, however, as you can write a scene without dialogue). Dialogue is the most obvious way to "show," because it brings your reader right into a visual situation, with banter and tone and body language (if you remember to write these things in). Dialogue lends itself to character development, too, but you have to re-member to show. We can't tell you how many students we've worked with who've included scenes in their memoirs where people are talking but not actually saying anything. ("Hi. How are you?" "Oh, fine. Great day, huh?") Yes, people talk like that, but it does nothing to advance your story, and it's bor-ing for the reader. In order to create a solid scene, you want to write dialogue that sounds real *and* shows something sig-nificant being exchanged without lots of exposition. This is a little bit like patting your head and rubbing your stomach and jumping up and down all at once—it's confusing at first, and not easy to master—but you'll get good at it after a while. As with most things, it just takes practice.

Conflict is another important component of scenes. A lot of dramatic-writing teachers will tell you that you must have a conflict in every scene—and a lot of writers, upon hearing this, balk at the idea, because conflict sounds unpleasant. But, as we said in Chapter 3, conflict does not have to be a car accident or people fighting. It can be as simple as one char-acter saying, "Hey, want to go get an ice cream?" and another character responding, "No, I don't. I hate the way it feels on my teeth."

This is a silly example, but it shows two people who aren't in agreement; the difference they're having may be minor, but it's still conflict. Essentially, as long as you're focusing on how people are interacting, what is happening, and what you, the protagonist, are doing and feeling in a given scene, you'll be executing elements of craft that will make for better, fuller, and more engaging scenes.

People tend to get a little bit overwhelmed by all of this. It's a lot to hold, and there's a steep learning curve. It's interesting—we work with a lot of people, especially high achievers, who think that they should just have this figured out, like either you're put on this planet to be a good writer or you're not. But that's just not true. The most successful writers are not necessarily the most innately talented; rather, they're the ones who are the most disciplined, who are eager to learn, who practice their craft, and who seek out help and support. We encourage you not to get frustrated with yourself and not to feel as if you're not good enough or that you'll never figure this stuff out—because it's just a question of time and effort. We've seen countless people have that "click" moment when all of a sudden they "get" scene writing and start doing it quite well. The "click" moment of learning is very profound, and it can happen for anyone who works hard enough for it.

PLOT

Most people understand what plot means. Anyone who's ever watched a movie understands the importance of plot, and anyone who's ever taken an English class (even if only in elementary school) has almost certainly spent some time talking about it.

Where many memoirists run into trouble, however, is that they tend to forget that plot is just as important in a memoir as it is in a novel. It's the engine that drives the story, and it's a causal result of action. But because we're telling our own stories, we tend to think that the most important thing to do is to stick to the facts of what happened—that even if telling the truth and nothing but the truth slows or disrupts the trajectory of our books, we have no alternative but to include everything relevant. That does not work when you're creating a focused story. As a memoirist, you have to make some hard decisions, specifically around cutting things that maybe are not necessary to your plot. And, equally important, you will have to choose where you need to take some creative license in order to improve your story.

One place where memoirists have some flexibility is in creating composites of people or places. If you had three aunts, for example, but it would serve the story better to have only one aunt as a central character, you could combine their personalities to make one aunt; or you could combine two different towns into one, or two similar experiences, for the same reason. This is not the same as fictionalizing, because you're not "making up" anything. You are writing what we call the "essential" truth, or emotional truth, even if what's on the page is not an exact depiction of absolute fact. Let's say, for example, that your parents divorced when you were young, so throughout your childhood you spent two nights a week at your dad's house and five nights a week at your mom's, and you remember those times of packing up on a Sunday but have trouble separating out each Sunday from the others. You can write about one particular Sunday anyway, but pull from your memory about all Sundays. You turn what you have at your disposal into a scene with dialogue and action—which doesn't make what you're writing any less true to your experience.

We worked with one client recently who said that all of her current scenes—the "today" scenes—were fun to write and were coming along quite nicely because she remembered them so well, but all of her flashback scenes were painful to write because she didn't remember every single detail. She hated feeling like she had to make things up. Her dilemma stuck with us, because we know there are solutions that we want to share with writers. Writing about what you don't remember well can and should be freeing to you as you dig into the details of how the moment felt in your body, how you remember it affecting your life. As long as you're sticking to your emotional truth, you're on the right path.

As you continue down this path, you have two ways to move your plot forward: through dialogue and sensory details, and through narrative summary—both of which comprise your scenes. Dialogue and sensory details tend to show more, while narrative summary is more about telling. In order to have a great memoir, you have to have a balance of the two, though the "show" should probably take a little more of the pie (around 60 percent, compared with telling, which should be about 40 percent, in our opinion). A scene is composed of not only dialogue, sensory details, and narrative summary but also takeaway, which we'll be discussing more in Chapter

5. There is a lot to hold in any given scene, which is why your toolbox is a nice image to think about. You have a lot of tools at your disposal, and you might not use all of them for each scene. Eventually you'll learn to pick and choose what feels right to you in a given moment, and the balance will start to feel like second nature to you. In the beginning, don't fret if you feel a little stuck or overwhelmed. Keep plugging along with the knowledge that every writer has to have a first draft in order to refine second and third drafts. You'll hit your pace soon enough.

THROUGH-THREADS

We use a lot of different images to talk about the use of through-threads. Sometimes we talk about it as planting a seed; sometimes we talk about it as wrapping a gift. Brooke's favorite analogy for through-threads, however, is the loom. When you look at a tapestry or rug that a loom has created, you realize that even if the person who made it has used hundreds of different colors, the colors always repeat themselves. If you find red in one place, you'll find it again somewhere else, even if the pattern is chaotic, because that single thread must resurface at some given point—unless the weaver intentionally cuts it off. This is, to us, exactly what it means to have a through-thread in a manuscript. If you introduce a through-thread—if you decide you're going to use red or blue or green or whatever you're going to use—it must reappear in your manuscript, and it's ultimately more gratifying if it shows up more than once or twice, even more so if you can follow it through to the end. If you drop that thread entirely, you have a problem. Anton Chekhov has been quoted as having written, "If you say in the first chapter that there is a rifle hanging on the wall, in the second or third chapter it absolutely must go off. If it's not going to be fired, it shouldn't be hanging there."

All this talk of colors and threads (and loaded rifles) probably feels a bit abstract, so let's get more specific with some examples. One memoir Brooke worked on when she was at Seal Press—a beautiful memoir by Chana Wilson called *Riding Fury Home*—starts when the author is about five years old and brings her all the way through to middle age. In her early draft, Wilson mentioned a dog that she got when she was maybe six or seven that was a very healing presence in her life. The dog was an important character around Chapter 5 or 6, and then that was it. The dog never came back. By the time Brooke was finished with Chapter 20 and the author was now in her late twenties, she started to worry: *What the hell happened to the dog?* So Brooke asked the author what happened—and it turned out that the dog had died when she was a teenager. The author couldn't believe that she'd left that out—but of course, for her, the dog's existence took a backseat to other, more tumultuous elements of her life during those years. The dog was important to Brooke as a reader, though, and not knowing what happened to it felt like an enormous hole in the story.

This is an example of a thing—in this case, a pet—being a through-thread, but through-threads are oftentimes concepts as well. In The *Glass Castle*, the concept of the "glass castle" itself is a through-thread. It's symbolic because it's a promise the author's father makes that someday they will live in a glass castle. Meanwhile, in reality, they live in abject poverty, and the glass castle, which starts as a dream of something marvelous for the future, ultimately turns into a symbol of betrayal, letdown, and neglect. It's something the author comes to resent, and it shows up in several scenes throughout the book, including when her father is on his deathbed.

It's important to note that through-threads are not the same thing as foreshadowing. They're simply important pieces of the story that you need to remember to mention again, or that you want to continue to bring up at various points in your story. The more you can try to introduce some through-threads that are symbolic in nature, the better. You might have a handful of them that you sprinkle throughout your book, and they can serve the deep and satisfying purpose of bringing your story full circle. This is about more than just attending to something you might have introduced and then forgotten to talk about later. For instance, early on in *Eat, Pray, Love*, Elizabeth Gilbert discovers an Italian word that she loves— *attraversiamo*, which means "to cross over." She's fascinated with what it symbolizes, as well as with the fact that there's no English equivalent of it. She ruminates on this word in several places throughout the book, and she uses it as an ultimate through-thread when she ends the book by saying the word *attraversiamo* to her lover, making it clear that she's going to take a chance on him—she's going to "cross over" with him. For readers, this is a very satisfying through-thread, as we feel as if we've been let in on something intimate and personal to Gilbert that has meaning to us as readers as well, because we've been instructed from an early point in the word's significance.

Now, you're not always going to go into writing your memoir thinking, *Oh, this is something that I want to be a through-thread.* Sometimes these patterns emerge organically as you go. This is where the metaphor of planting a seed comes in. When you plant a seed, you need to tend to it as it grows and eventually harvest it. It has its own life span. The hard part, of course, can be figuring out what is a seed and what isn't. And you have to be careful, because not every single thing you introduce is going to be a thread. Some things are just landscape or scenery, and you need to be able to identify the difference.

One way we suggest identifying through-threads is to print out your chapters as you finish them and put them in a binder. Then go through with a highlighter and mark the themes and topics that you feel you should come back to later—loops you will need to close at some point. As you do this, create a running list of the through-threads you're finding so you have them all in one place. Then, midway through your memoir, you can go through your list and revisit those highlighted passages and figure out whether you've closed all the loops you've created. (You'll want to do this again when you reach the end of your memoir, but it's good to check up on yourself at the halfway point.)

There will be times when you won't be able to close some of those loops within the scope of your narrative. In Linda Joy's memoir, for example, there are people who are really important from an emotional standpoint when she's young, but then they move away or nobody hears about them for many years. She left those characters unattended in her first edition, even though she recognized that this left a hole in her story. When she wrote her revised edition, she decided she wanted to give readers some sort of resolution regarding those characters, so she included an epilogue in which she explained what happened to them. If you can't tie off all of your through-threads within the story itself, an epilogue that brings the reader up to speed is a great alternative to prevent your story from ending up with a bunch of loose ends.

Even if you utilize these techniques, there will be some through-threads (like Chana Wilson's dog) that will slip through the cracks. We spend a lot of time fixing through-thread issues in the manuscripts we work on, in fact. (Luckily, a good editor who's paying attention will generally catch them.) But if you make tending to your through-threads a conscious decision—if you make it a point to be intentional with them from the very beginning—then hopefully your readers will never have to ask themselves, *Wait, what happened to that?*

TRANSPARENCY & RELATABILITY

We can't talk about writing memoir without talking about transparency and relatability, and the important roles each one plays in your success as a writer of personal prose. Many writers we've worked with have trouble being transparent and relatable—not because they don't want to be, but because they're afraid to reveal too much and/or they've arrived at a staid place in their writing without even realizing it. The problem is, if you don't reveal enough to your readers, they will have no reason to care about you or your story.

Part of being transparent and relatable has to do with voice; part of it has to do with opening yourself up to be your 100 percent authentic self. And it's understandable that so many authors are fearful of this idea: you have to make yourself vulnerable, and that's a scary thing to do. You may have to share things that feel uncomfortable to share. But in order to have a truly knock-it-out-of-the-park memoir, you do need to feel uncomfortable sometimes. Not all the time, by any means, but sometimes, yes. If none of the writing you've done so far has made you feel uncomfortable, then we would challenge you to do some writing that does make you feel that way. You need to walk the radical edge of your writing in order to test your outer boundaries, to see how far you can push, and to know what in fact feels like going too far. Some writers never even get close to that outer boundary because they're playing it too safe, and the effect on those people's writing is pretty transparent: there's not much depth there. If you stay entirely in your comfort zone from beginning to conclusion, you're not showing up wholly and authentically, and if you're not showing up 100 percent, your audience will see that, and you will lose them.

For many writers, their discomfort with the idea of sharing personal experiences, feelings, and thoughts with their audience stems from the fact that they have trouble trusting their inner wisdom or accepting that their truths are also other people's truths. The concept of offering universalisms is overwhelming to them. But universalisms don't have to be these big, important, philosophical ideas or lightning-strike moments of enlightenment; they're just points where you can choose to meet your reader. That's it. You just need to reach down into your own knowingness and give yourself permission to tell your truth.

There is a flip side to this: some people are so transparent and have so little shame around anything that they actually overshare, which can also alienate readers. This can especially happen around bodily issues and sex. If you're writing erotica or a book that's specifically about sex, then maybe there isn't such a thing as going too far—but you have to know your genre, and if being intensely graphic isn't part of it, you may need to exercise some restraint. Transparency is not the same as giving every single detail about everything; it's showing up with an aliveness. It's being who you are when you interact with someone you really like—when you show up and you're on and engaged and completely present. At the 2014 Wake Up

Festival, put on by the publisher Sounds True, Tami Simon, the founder, said that authentically sharing something that matters to you always leads to universal truth. This is exactly what we're pointing to here. Your authentic truth is the voice that you want to bring to your memoir no matter what you're writing about—the hard stuff or the easy stuff.

Bringing this energy to the page requires digging into what you think and feel. So even if you're writing about something really tough—a tragic experience that you had in childhood, for example—you've got to write it almost like you're having coffee with a good friend and telling them about this really hard thing that happened to you. All the emotions that would surface in such a conversation are what you need to bring to the page. Otherwise, even if you provide a lot of information and facts and include wonderful scene setting and dialogue, your reader will have no sense of how you *feel* about any of it—which means they won't be able to connect with what you're writing, and they will fall out of the fictive dream.

We see memoirists leave their feelings out of their writing all the time. Sometimes they do it on purpose—because they think it's too much telling, or because they assume the reader knows how they feel, or because they think it's implied. Sometimes they're bored with themselves or worried that their readers will be bored, though the irony here, of course, is that we are bored when someone does not let us see their full expression of self. Sometimes writers simply fail to bring their full authentic selves to bear because they're not in touch with their emotions, or because they're so nervous around their emotions that they avoid them altogether, consciously or subconsciously. If you're one of these writers, try to find a way to get those emotions out in your writing. Yes, you do have to make assumptions sometimes that your readers are going to understand what you're talking about without your having to spell it all out; you don't want to talk down to your audience, after all. But you can't always take for granted that your readers will be right there with you without a little help. They're reading your story, but they're not in your head—or, rather, they won't be until you let them in.

The reason all of the truly best-selling memoirs out there are as popular as they are is that the authors make you feel like you really know them. They invite you into their world in a way that makes you feel like you've just spent quality time with them when you leave it. And this should be one of your goals as a memoirist: to invite someone into your world and, once they're there, to make them like you—without trying too hard, that is. This may seem like a no-brainer, but we've worked with some writers who (inadvertently, of course) have said things in their memoirs that are elitist, dismissive, or alienating in some way. You don't want to curb your language—you want to be fully authentic—but you do need to be conscientious about how you're going to be perceived. And this requires a fair amount of self-awareness. In the end, your reader has to like you enough to want to read 80,000 words of your writing. And it's not going to happen because you've left out the more unsavory aspects of your life and character. They will connect even more with you because you've gone through some sort of transformation in the course of your story, and they have accompanied you through it. You've kept them engaged and invested in your story, and now they care about you and identify with your struggle as if it were their own. You have taken them on a journey of self-discovery, which is the best kind of writing you can offer.

ONE BITE AT A TIME

As we discussed at the beginning of this chapter, craft is an area where many writers get a little bit confused. As you write, you begin to wonder, *How much is enough? How do I know what to include and what to leave out?* Unfortunately, there's no stock answer for that; you have to feel your way into it by experimenting, writing, revising, and writing some more. For many writers, this is a lifelong journey. The memoir you're writing right now won't necessarily take your whole life—but odds are, this isn't the only book, or even the only memoir, you'll ever write. Once the memoir bug has bitten you, it's a hard thing to shake.

The criticism memoirists probably hear more often than any other is that memoir is nothing more than an exercise in navel-gazing. It can be. But it doesn't *have* to be. Don't let the fear of being called self-indulgent or narcissistic silence you. Remember, if you put too much on the page, you can always remove, revise, and rewrite it. It's better to say too much in your early drafts and pull back on the reins a bit later than it is to say too little to begin with. Ultimately, the real energy behind a good memoir—the reason people write their stories for an audience in the first place—is the exact opposite of self-indulgence. It's like trial by fire. It's painful. It's a baring of the soul. It's probably one of the most powerful things you'll ever do. And if you immerse your readers in your story—if you can use all of the tools at your disposal to really make a connection with your audience—it will make a real difference in other people's lives.

CHAPTER 5:

Finishing Touches

The human brain reacts instantly to sensory details, which is why, as a writer, you need to know how to create a world your reader will engage with both emotionally and viscerally. Sensual details bring your story alive and offer your reader a way to feel your story, to—as we discussed in Chapter 4—"light up" their brain with your experiences.

For most of us, it's not until after we've finished a first full draft that we will begin to add in these extra nuances. It's like we're painters who have finished filling the canvas with the necessary background, and now we're going back in to layer on the additional elements to make our painting leap out at the viewer. The basics are there, and now it's time to dress up our prose and make it more attractive to our readers.

We want to encourage you to understand that a memoir is multilayered, and that yours will not be complete once you're finished with your first draft. Even after you "finish" your manuscript, it will still likely need a few more passes. This is the purpose of this chapter—to cover the things that you might not even think much about until your first draft is done and you're making your later passes.

SENSUAL DETAILS

As you read (or even transcribe) other memoirists' stories, you may feel at times as if you're living their experiences. And this what stories do: they allow us to simulate an intense experience without actually having to live through it. We talked a bit about this in Chapter 4 when we went over writing scenes, but let's dig in even deeper here. We're all immersed in stories from the time we're young. Think about your earliest memories: Do you remember where you were? When it was? What you were smelling in that moment (perhaps flowers, or perfume, or something cooking)? If you have any memories like that, thinking about them can help clue you in to what we're talking about here. In order to fully communicate that memory to someone else—to make them experience it the way you did—you would have to convey all the different elements of your experience: the sight, the smell, the sound, the feel. To do anything short of that might give them a vague sense of what that moment was like for you, but it wouldn't allow them to *live* it the way you did.

A wonderful moment from *Wired for Story* is where Lisa Cron writes about the universal story: "The universal is the portal that allows us to climb into the skin of characters completely different from us and feel what they feel," she explains. "What's ironic is that only when embodied in the specifics of a story does the universal become accessible." That's exactly it: only in drilling down to the small details do you locate the commonality of your experiences with others. And that's why being specific in your scenes—"dropping into" your scenes, so it's as if you're there in that moment—is so important.

Let's look at a couple of examples of what this looks like, starting with an excerpt from the very beginning of Cheryl Strayed's memoir, *Wild*:

> *The trees were tall, but I was taller, standing above them on a steep mountain slope in northern California. Moments before, I'd removed my hiking boots and the left one had fallen into those trees, first catapulting into the air when my enormous backpack toppled onto it, then skittering across the gravelly trail and flying over the edge. It bounced off of a rocky outcropping several feet beneath me before disappearing into the forest canopy below, impossible to retrieve. I let out a stunned gasp, though I'd been in the wilderness thirty-eight days and by then I'd come to know that anything could happen and that everything would. But that doesn't mean I wasn't shocked when it did.*

This is wonderful because there is some action going on in this scene, but what really makes the moment arresting is the sensual detail Strayed includes. You get specifics about where she is—on a trail, surrounded by trees—and you get these great verbs: "catapulting," "toppled," "skittering," "flying," "bounced." We are in this moment with her—we feel like we're standing alongside her, feeling that same sense of shock she is as she watches her boot disappear into the trees below.

. . . .

Transcribing Your Way to Brilliancy

Most people write memoir because they have a story to tell, or because they have to—there's no *not* writing memoir for some. A lot of people also write because they fell in love with reading as kids and want to emulate those great writers they knew and loved—and, of course, those great writers had vivid imaginations and wrote beautiful stories. There's no reason that your memoir can't be every bit as beautiful and imaginative as those stories you treasured as a child. The memoirs we've referred to throughout this book are all bursting with lovely, evocative language—with those moments that make you stop reading a passage so you can savor it. You can't believe that someone has written such an amazingly perfect sentence.

When Brooke was in San Miguel de Allende, Mexico

in 2013 for the annual writers' conference there, Cheryl Strayed was one of the keynote speakers for the week. She spoke about how she spent time teaching herself to become a better writer by transcribing the writers whom she loved. She copied their work, word for word, and then, once she had a feel for it, tried to emulate their style in her own writing.

Since then, we've talked to various writers about this idea, and some have tried it and found it quite transformative. It's incredible to see what people come back with after this exercise. So if you're someone who struggles with "flat" writing, go ahead and try this: pick a memoir you love and transcribe even just a couple of pages, then return to your own writing and attempt to mimic the other book's style. You may be surprised by the results.

. . . .

Here's another excerpt of a scene, this one from Linda Joy's memoir, *Don't Call Me Mother*:

> The landscape is dotted with derricks whose steel arms pump oil up through layers of time. The whole town smells of oil. I stand outside to listen to the wind blowing the spirit of the past against my pale body. Dirt from an ancient era blows against me. I bow my head to the power of the land, the wind lifting my hair and

tickling my skin with pinpricks of bone too small to be seen with the naked eye.

What Linda Joy did here was to create a sense of place and time, giving specific details—the smell, the look, the feel—and also to offer a sense of the themes she's about to explore. You have dirt against bare legs; you have the wind tickling her skin; you have a sense of what she's experiencing as a young girl in an Oklahoma town. She brings the moment alive so you feel like you're right there with her. This is the power of sensual details.

DIALOGUE

For memoir writers, creating dialogue can be a daunting prospect. We are always hearing questions like, "I don't remember what people said so many years ago, so how can I create true dialogue? That would be fictionalizing." Or, "I don't know how to write dialogue. Do I have to?"

We hope we can put your mind at ease at bit here, because although we believe that dialogue is a necessary element of story writing, we also know that anyone can learn how to create enough dialogue; it just takes practice. In a memoir, you have to translate the essence of what you remember through a particular scene. Of course, none of us walks through life carrying a tape recorder, so dialogue is a place where we must re-create, to the best of our memories, the essence of what people were saying in particular circumstances. Memoir is made of significant moments in scenes that *show* characters, events, and moments of meaning and tension. You no doubt remember the feelings you had at that time, so your job is to tap into the essence of what happened, recalling it to the best of your ability, and then to create dialogue to show that in scene. Rest assured that you are bringing the emotional truth of what happened to the page. Most of what you write will not be verbatim what people said, especially if you're writing a scene from twenty or thirty years ago, but as long as you are writing dialogue as it would have happened—or must have happened, based on your memory of it—you are not fictionalizing.

There are a few "rules" of dialogue to keep in mind. The first is that the purpose of dialogue is to show character and personality. Dialogue is a way to present how people speak, act, and react, to show layers of personality and character. It exists to reveal how people talk and to portray their attitude, background, culture, and education through the way they talk.

In response to "Would you like dessert?" someone might respond, "Yes, please, I'd love some," or, "Sure, pile it on right here, darlin," or, "Can't never get enough a dat, can ya?" or, "Thank you so much, dear, for your consideration." Each of these responses comes from a different kind of person, quickly characterized in a single sentence of dialogue.

You can choose direct dialogue, shown in quotation marks, like the above examples, or indirect dialogue, in which what is said is stated by you, the author. This example shows both direct and indirect dialogue:

"Can you please tell me the way to the Golden Gate Bridge?" the bald man in the Mercedes asked me.

I told him to go three blocks and turn left, hoping he'd get lost.

Too often, beginning writers do dialogue "on the nose." Instead of using indirect dialogue, they might write in response, *"Go three blocks and turn left." I hoped he'd get lost.*

It's not wrong to do this, but by using indirect dialogue, you save words and vary your sentence construction as well.

What follows is another trap writers often get into—what we call "talking heads," a long exchange of dialogue with no tags or body language. This kind of writing, we find, also has no purpose or meaning other than to show friends meeting up. There needs to be a reason to use dialogue—generally because it's characterizing a person in your memoir or because it furthers the scene in some way.

"Hi, Joanie, it's been a long time."

"Yes, it's good to see you, too."

"What have you been up to?"

"Oh, not much. As you can see, I'm busy with the baby."

"Well, it was good to see you."

"You too."

This is a very simplistic passage, but we see material like this all the time—writing that includes no body language and no real points of interest. Here's how that passage might be rewritten:

I saw Joanie and the baby coming from down the block, and there was no escaping her. She'd already seen me and put on a big smile as I greeted her.

"Joanie, it's been a long time."

She kept smiling but did a little dance beside the baby carriage as she said, "Good to see you, too."

I didn't know what else to say, embarrassed that I hadn't sent her a card when the baby was born. I just didn't know how to handle it, since I knew who the baby's father was but didn't know if she knew that I knew. To cover up my nervousness I asked her what she'd been doing, but all she could do was gesture toward the baby and grin with a kind of nervous tic, as if that explained everything. We made small talk until finally I checked my cell phone and told her I had to go. All that sweet pleasantness gave me a stomachache as I walked on, determined not to look back.

When the author includes thoughts, body language, and indirect dialogue, we can see that there's a reason this scene belongs in the memoir. We can detect the tension in the pleasantries that these two characters share, and their discomfort during this exchange, as well as some obvious history that makes us want to keep reading.

The best way to handle dialogue is to listen to how people talk. Most of the time, ordinary speech includes meaningless comments, grunts, and "mmms" that we leave out when we write, but you can learn to listen to how people phrase things, and the various kinds of language and rhythms of speech that people use. Get a cup of coffee and eavesdrop on a few conversations at a coffeehouse. Write down the exchanges. This will give you a feel for a range of conversational patterns. Notice how people talk in movies. Dialogue in movies does several things at once: advances the plot, shows character, and creates tension. That is good storytelling. And, importantly, read good fiction and other memoirs and notice how other writers use these techniques. You might even take our advice from the sidebar above and copy some passages to get a feel for the use of quotation marks and commas and the proper way to create dialogue exchanges.

Another important tip is to read your dialogue out loud. If you can, ask a friend or family member to read other characters' parts, to get a sense of how it feels when it's spoken out loud. In time, you'll start to tune your ear differently, and after enough practice, it will start to come naturally to you.

METAPHOR, SIMILE, AND ANALOGY

Metaphor, simile, and analogy are some of the building blocks you might use to create these beautiful sentences we're talking about, to add in those sensual details. In using these devices, you invite the reader to use their imagination—to step completely outside of their comfort zone or to picture things that are outrageous or exaggerated or fun or wild. When you fail to use them at all, your writing runs the danger of falling a bit flat.

Let's do a little bit of English 101 here, just in case it's been a while since you've thought about metaphor, simile, and analogy. A metaphor is a figure of speech in which a word or phrase is applied to an object or action to which it is not literally applicable—"She is my sun," for example. A simile is a specific type of metaphor that compares one thing with another thing of a different kind, used to make a description more emphatic or vivid, that uses "like" or "as" to make the comparison—"That man is sly like a fox," for example. An analogy, meanwhile, is a comparison between two things that have something in common, usually for the purpose of explanation or clarification—"A heart is like a pump," for example.

Together, these three devices have the ability to evoke something for readers that straightforward description can't. Metaphors in particular can be exciting, because they invite you to think about something as directly compared to something else that it could never be; they ask you to suspend disbelief the most. But all three of these devices crook a finger at the reader and ask them to join you on your journey.

Going back to *Wild*, we find some wonderful examples of metaphor and analogy in Strayed's writing, including in her description of the backpack she wears during her hike along the Pacific Crest Trail. "It was officially attached to me," she writes. "It seemed like a Volkswagen Beetle, only now it seemed like a Volkswagen Beetle that was parked on my back." So that is a simile (and a good simile, at that). In an earlier place in the manuscript, right before she begins her trek, she describes trying to heft the bag onto her back, and she says, "It was exactly like attempting to lift a Volkswagen Beetle." Here, then, we actually have an analogy—she's offering up the weight of a VW Beetle for comparison so we understand just how heavy the backpack felt to her in that moment.

We have two places here where a backpack is being compared to a car, and in one case it's a simile, and in one it's an analogy. It's important to recognize the distinction there when you're looking at it, as a lot of people get confused about the difference. Remember, a simile always has "like" or "as" in it, but that doesn't mean that *all* sentences containing one of those words are similes. For instance, if you were to say, "For me, going to the grocery store is like pulling teeth," you're comparing going grocery shopping to going to the dentist— you're making an analogy between the two activities in order to convey just how much you dislike food shopping. Strive to understand the nuances here, because analogy is often unde-rused in memoir, and it can go a long way toward engaging and connecting your reader with your story.

One of the things we frequently talk about in the courses we teach is the concept of overlaying. You aren't necessarily going to be able to use a lot of metaphor, simile, and analogy in your early drafts; you may need to start with just your plot, or your characters, or the skeletons of your scenes. And that's okay—in fact, if trying to use these devices is going to slow you down or distract you from the meat of what you're trying to communicate, you should steer clear of them initially. But later, when your foundation is down, your drywall is up, and your roof is on, then you get to play and have fun with the decorating. This is a good time to revisit the final chapter of this book, as so much of what we're writing about here will happen after the first—or even second—draft of your book is complete.

When you think about these devices in this way—as decoration—you realize that they're just imaginative sprinklings of detail, stuff that can be added into your manuscript at any time. You can wait until you have a full first draft down if you want to, and then you can read through the whole thing, looking just for metaphor, simile, and analogy, making notes about where you might layer them in. Remember, if you set out to find something very specific, then it's likely that you're going to. If you approach your yard, and the lawn is totally overgrown, and you're not looking for anything in particular, you're probably going to see a lot of different things and not really know what to tend to. But if you go out into your yard and think, *I'm looking for dandelions* or, *I'm looking for snails*, then you're going to find those things, because your mind is attuned to them. It's the same thing with your manuscript: when you have a full manuscript and you get to this point of decorating, you can say, *I'm going to tune my brain and all of my attention and all of my sensory efforts toward adding metaphor, simile, and analogy*—and it will come more easily than you might think.

. . . .

What Do You Do When You're Not Good at Metaphors, Similes, and Analogies?

Some writers we work with have told us, "I'm just not good at metaphor, simile, and analogy; every time I try, it sounds awkward, it sounds clunky—it just doesn't work." This generally comes from people who don't think of themselves as creative, but really, it's usually a case of your inner critic piping up and interfering with your work.

What we suggest if you're one of these people is to go through your manuscript once it's written and mark, with a highlighter or some kind of symbol, places where a metaphor, simile, or analogy might be helpful. Then, once you have marked these places, either you can start playing with possibilities yourself (there are some great, easy-to-find practice resources online), or, if you really just don't think these things are your forte and need some help, you might consider inviting over creative friends for a metaphor party. Read the surrounding sentences, and ask everyone to brainstorm with you. It's fun, and you'll be amazed by what great ideas can come out of it!

. . . .

THROUGH-THREADS REVISITED

We know we covered through-threads in Chapter 4, but just as they're important to return to again and again within your manuscript, they're something we want to circle back to here. This is because, like metaphor, simile, and analogy, they are something you may not necessarily layer in until you're in the thick of revisions, after you already have a first or even second draft completed.

In tending to your through-threads, you acknowledge that the reader has been on the journey *with* you, and that there are things you might have talked about early on in the manuscript that you want to recall or further develop. Essentially, you're rewarding your reader for paying attention.

We mentioned in the last chapter that we sometimes describe using through-threads as being like wrapping a present: by this we mean it's something that you have to finish once you've started it. You have to make all the right folds and tape the sides and then tie the ribbon across the package. You wouldn't bring a half-wrapped package with an untied ribbon to a party, right? Well the same goes for your memoir:

don't present your reader with a story that doesn't have all its through-threads cleaned up. Make sure everything is "fully wrapped," by which we mean that these moments of opportunity to satisfy your reader by attending to the small details are taken into consideration and well executed.

As we said before, you may have to tie off some of your through-threads in your epilogue; sometimes the wrap-up just doesn't fit within the scope of your story. But often you'll have the opportunity to put the finishing touches on your through-threads—to tie that bow—before the end of your story. And when you have that opportunity, you need to seize it. True, sometimes these threads can be difficult to see, but if you're answering the questions you set out for yourself at the beginning of the journey, you shouldn't lose your way.

TAKEAWAY

It's appropriate to end our book on takeaway, because takeaway is what a reader leaves with when they're finished with a book. It's what sticks with them emotionally, and what agents, editors, and publishers are looking for when they're deciding what memoirs they want to take on and publish. Takeaway, at the most basic level of understanding, is reflection. It's how you make sense of the experiences that you've shared with the readers through your scenes, and it often points to some sort of universal message.

Takeaway is often difficult for writers to wrap their minds

around. We've worked with many memoirists who simply don't feel they can do takeaway, and we've seen countless memoirs that simply don't have any. But all good memoir must have takeaways, because, as Brooke likes to say, in the takeaways are the kernels of truth and insight that pierce the heart of the reader. Takeaways are the mirror, the moments where the writer is saying, "Yes, we're the same, because we're human." Your upbringing might have been very different from that of the person who's reading your memoir. Your life experiences are obviously wholly your own. But the emotional connection we are capable of making with our readers transcends experience. We all know grief, loss, suffering, happiness, elation, frustration. It doesn't mean that your reader has to have experienced what you've experienced in order to relate to you. We've read books about child loss, addiction, sexual abuse, world travel, weight loss, rehab, and many other topics that are incredibly *relatable*, regardless of whether we've experienced what the authors have experienced. The books' appeal stems from the authors' capacity to tap into the universal human emotions of their unique journeys.

Takeaway can sometimes be your own summary of your experience, one that makes sure to reflect on why something mattered or what you learned. It can also look like philosophizing, where you draw a bigger-picture conclusion about something. Caroline Knapp, in *Drinking, A Love Story*, employs this technique in every chapter of her book. In writing about a woman she knows who suffers from insecurity,

Knapp writes, "This is such a universal female experience, the lack of self-worth and the rage that simmers underneath it." This single sentence serves as a takeaway for the reader because she pulls away from speaking about her friend and turns this woman's insecurity outward, onto all women, onto the reader. And the reader relates—or at least most will. And this is another secret of takeaway. You must risk that what you say will be experienced as truth, regardless of those who may not relate to you. You have to risk making statements and owning your own expertise, and not be afraid of making conclusions.

Many memoirists we work with discover in working with us that they don't do takeaways because they don't trust their own wisdom. Takeaway requires you to observe, to opine, to state something that you believe to be true. We encourage you not to worry about those people who might object. There will always be objectors; that does not mean they can deny your truth, or your experience, or what you know in your heart, and what you have to impart to your readers. What calls most memoirists to write is the message they want to leave their readers with—and that message is at the heart of takeaway. You must gradually learn to do this and to effectively draw conclusions about your own experience if you want your reader to walk away with some sense of meaning from your book. (And a quick note to writers who are doing coming-of-age memoirs: takeaway can come through your characters, too. Sometimes children don't have the wisdom or the depth of experience to be able to offer these universal truths, but the adults that you're writing about surely do—and we taught about how both Jeannette Walls and Frank McCourt did this effectively in their memoirs, *The Glass Castle* and *Angela's Ashes*, respectively.)

In order to start to wrap your mind around takeaway, read memoirs with an eye for those moments that pierce your heart, when the author pulls away from personal experience and into something more global. If you're uncomfortable with reflection, test it out little by little. See if you can start to integrate it into your work in small bites. Takeaway can be quite formulaic if you want it to be, and that doesn't make it wrong. By this we mean that you can always do your takeaways at the end of a scene, or at the end of a chapter. You don't have to be adept at weaving them throughout your book and in the middle of scenes for them to be effective. But trust us that your reader will have a more heartfelt experience if you can learn to train an eye to the power of the takeaway. We hope, if you're not doing it already, that you'll give takeaway a try.

Thank You, And An Offer

Well, you made it to the end, and we hope that you've gained some valuable ideas and insights for your memoir project that you'll be able to integrate into your writing practice. There is so much to learn and to figure out on this journey, and it's about so much more than becoming a better writer, or even publishing your memoir. The journey you're on is about you—coming into your own, claiming your space as a memoir writer, and hopefully, ultimately, writing and publishing more, whether that's on your blog, online, in personal pieces for publication, or in another memoir.

We recommend that you revisit this book and other books on writing over and over again as you write. Some aspects of what we cover here will resonate more deeply during particular points in your process as you practice and experiment and grow as a writer. You can't master everything at once, so also be gentle with yourself around those areas that might feel more difficult than others. And know that certain things will need to simply be turned over—maybe to an editor or a coach or someone who can help you connect with a deeper "click" moment about something that might feel particularly elusive. That's okay, too. Your story is and will still be wholly your own.

We want to thank you for reading our book by offering you a gift—a download of our course "What Made *Wild* (by Cheryl Strayed) a Best-Selling Memoir?" (The direct link can be accessed at http://www.writeyourbookinsixmonths. com/free-wild.) Please follow this unique link to get this gift ($29.95 value). We'll also stay in touch with you about future classes, and offer ongoing insight and support around your memoir writing. We encourage you to find us online via social media as well (the links to which you'll find on the About the Authors page of this book), and to stay in touch.

Thanks for reading!
Linda Joy & Brooke

About the Authors

LINDA JOY MYERS, PhD, is president and founder of the National Association of Memoir Writers and has been a therapist for thirty-five years. Her memoir, *Don't Call Me Mother: A Daughter's Journey from Abandonment to Forgiveness,* is a finalist for the ForeWord Book of the Year Award and a finalist for the Indie Excellence Awards and received Honorable Mention from the New York Book Awards. She's also the author of three books on memoir writing: *The Power of Memoir, Journey of Memoir,* and *Becoming Whole.*

BROOKE WARNER is publisher of She Writes Press, president of Warner Coaching Inc., and author of *What's Your Book?* and *How to Sell Your Memoir*. Brooke's expertise is in traditional and new publishing, and she is an equal advocate for publishing with a traditional house and self-publishing. She sits on the board of the Independent Book Publishers Association (IBPA) and the National Association of Memoir Writers (NAMW). Her website was selected by The Write Life as one of the Top 100 Best Websites for Writers in 2014. She lives and works in Berkeley, California.

author photos © Reenie Raschke

FIND LINDA JOY ONLINE:

www.namw.org
www.memoriesandmemoirs.com
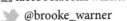 facebook.com/LindaJoyMyersAuthor
@memoirguru

FIND BROOKE ONLINE:

www.warnercoaching.com
www.shewritespress.com
facebook.com/warnercoaching
@brooke_warner